Commit to believing you deserve to experience all the love and connection your heart desires. No earning or repenting or serving time is required. (Elephants never forget this.)

" *Alice*

Sarah Seidelmann's

BORN TO

FREAK

a Salty Primer for

IRREPRESSIBLE
HUMANS

"Why everything you've been told is wrong with you is absolutely right with you!"

FIRST EDITION
ISBN 978-0-9882899-0-1
Printed in the USA

COVER CONCEPT BY
Kim Bagwill – The Frantic Meerkat
Artist/graphic designer/business owner who loves to
hunt and gather books, old photos, and ephemera to surround
herself with and inspire her paintings and graphic designs.

COVER AND INTERIOR BOOK DESIGN BY
Drai Bearwomyn – Wild Redhead Design
ADD mom/wife/womyn with manic/life-pirate/artist facets who
makes magic, sings, drums, gets things done using lists,
and is super proud to be part of this important book.

EDITED AND SHEPHERDED BY
Grace Kerina – The Writer's Shepherd
Highly sensing four-eyes nerd who moved to Germany with
two suitcases (one full of books) and who loves it that her
amazing clients help the world be sillier and healthier.

IMAGES
Used with permission by
Dover Publications, Inc.
and www.vintageprintable.com

For Alice and all of the other elephants

INTRODUCTION

Become stoked.
Frost your life cake.

"Alice

Introduction

First, I offer you a giant hug. Being born a FREAK isn't always easy, but I hope you'll see that it is amazing.

A FREAK is someone who was born to see things differently and to be an agent of change. Many of us who were born to FREAK arrived on Earth with heightened sensitivity and a certain irrepressibility. **Our FREAKY nature provides us with strange and often entirely original notions,** many of which aren't welcomed by our society, our culture, or the systems within which we work and live.

> You were born to FREAK.
> Embrace the fact that not everyone gets you.
>
> " *Alice*

And yet ... I believe our strange urgings, notions, sensitivities, and general irrepressibility always have and always will change and heal the world, making it ridiculously better.

Within this book you'll find an **A to Z primer of concepts** that can be mighty handy for a FREAK to press into service – perspectives I've learned that help me embrace and celebrate my FREAKY inner nature, with stories helpful to FREAKS on a path of greatness.

Like other FREAKS, I have **boatloads of unique and seemingly contradictory inner selves**. As a way to show how one FREAK's inner multitudes develop and cohabitate, in the "Allow Myself to Introduce Myself" bits of the book, you'll find stories about my wacky life and irrepressibility, as an offer of encouragement and (I hope) comic relief.

NOBODY messes with elephants.

" *Alice*

There is also within these pages a **large and wondrous pachyderm named Alice**. She enters bearing salty, elephantine wisdom in the form of commands and quips, meant to encourage and goad those of us who are born to FREAK. Alice is one of my greatest champions, and she welcomes the spotlight.

I came to the realization somewhat late in life that I was born to FREAK.

It is my dream that by confessing my own strangeness and sharing **tales of EPIC FREAKY awesomeness**, other irrepressible humans might get the memo earlier in their lives that they, too, were born to FREAK. I dream that the grandparent, parent, aunt, uncle, spouse, friend, or co-worker of a FREAK reads this book and so recognizes, celebrates, and encourages FREAKS in their own particular brand of greatness.

Not everyone can handle your awesomeness.
That's okay. Toss them a loving "Namaste"
and take your effervescence elsewhere.

" *Alice*

How do you know if you were born to FREAK? Well, that's a question for you to answer for yourself. My hunch is that if you've picked up this book, you can stop doubting it.

I wish you peace, love, and the awesome tenacity and unmatched courage of a hundred honey badgers.

Love,
Sarah

P.S. Please feel free to read this book in any order you darn well please — backwards, forwards, or browsing at random.

It's your born-to-FREAK prerogative to do it your way.

Exercise it!

OUR MULTITUDES

Celebrate the fact that your
MUCHNESS is what makes you
irresistible and connects you
powerfully to others.

"Alice

"Do I contradict myself?

Very well then I contradict myself,

(I am large, I contain multitudes.)"

—Walt Whitman

"Song of Myself"

It takes courage to share our wondrous facets with others, especially the facets that strongly contradict each other. The pathologist who likes to decoupage. The crusty orthopedic surgeon who likes to rescue puppies. The man who likes to dress as a woman. The stoic ornithologist who likes to decorate cakes. But it's these very contradictions that reflect our humanity. When we foster our perfect contradictions, our multitudes, we can make the world a better place.

Someone once said to me, "You're such an enigma. In some ways, you're kind of glamorous, worldly, and sophisticated, but in other ways you're so down-to-earth and silly and kind of a goofball." I'd heard similar comments in the past about me not being entirely consistent or coherent, and some of them took me by surprise (I don't, for example, feel particularly glamorous, worldly, or sophisticated). I used to think something was wrong with me for having such contradictory facets. But not any longer.

Of course I contradict myself. I am so many things and a lover of so much. I feel strangely drawn to high fashion, muddy trails, certain kinds of rap music, bread baking, Victorian natural history illustrations, ancient Vedic texts, babies, butterflies, India, Paris, and Minnesota. Of course I live and breathe contradictions – I was born to FREAK.

It excites me to imagine a world where all people allow their different facets to show. (He's a neat-as-a-pin accountant by day who cranks his red-hot bass guitar on a stage in the secret twilight hours.) Embracing these facets – and I'm not talking about the superficial ones – is what being truly alive is all about. These different parts of us yearn to be played out and with. I've learned that joyfully claiming personal contradictions helps make us whole and can bring genuine delight to other humans.

JESSEY'S MULTITUDES *Jessey, one of my dear friends, is a hilarious, coyote-like court jester, a Heyoka (the Lakota's concept of the sacred clown) of the highest order, especially when he's teaching a Pilates class and you're on one of those horrible devices they call "the reformer," with your bladder half full. You're being stretched and pulled in different directions, having cellular flashbacks to the dark times of the Inquisition, and all of a sudden Jessey unleashes a one-liner that causes you to shout obscenities and contract and stretch all at once. At which point, you*

> *a) pee,*
> *b) beg for mercy, or*
> *c) do both.*

Jessey can carry off wearing a full-on feathered headdress, sequins, and faux eyelashes. On the other hand, he can be a very serious, soulful, quiet intellectual who's well-read and has a firm grip on what it means to live intentionally. He's one of the most masterfully open and honest human beings I've met. His multitudes fascinate me. I love them.

Not long ago, a shamanic healing was performed on me by a rakish fellow-physician. The irony was that the last person I'd have thought I'd seek healing from was a male physician (especially a rakish one) ... yet it was, as are so many things in life, perfect.

The results of shamanic healing (see sidebar in "A is for ATTENTION DEFICIT"), which heals the spiritual aspect of disease, are often surprising, and yet discoveries made in a shamanic healing often feel settling and right, like mind-boggling truths.

I'd requested a healing about a thought that had been plaguing me – that I wouldn't be able to support myself financially by doing work I love (writing, speaking, healing). During the healing, the lovely physician-shaman retrieved a lost part of my soul for me.

SOUL LOSS *In the shamanic view of the world, our souls represent our essence, our life force, and we are born whole, with our souls intact. As we live our lives, certain situations, traumas, encounters, or experiences may cause parts of our souls to leave us. A bit of soul flees to a safe, peaceful place to avoid a painful experience. But without those parts of our souls, we can't operate with our full life force. We're not fully ourselves. We're not fully actualized. Shamanic practitioners know how to go on a journey, aided by helping spirits, to seek and retrieve the soul parts that have fled and ask them if they're willing to return. When soul parts return to us, our life force returns. It's empowering. According to some experts, soul loss is the most widespread cause of disease on the planet. It's really important to welcome, honor, and integrate all of our soul parts into our lives.*

As the physician-shaman and his helping spirits did their work on me, my missing soul part appeared to him in a vision as a babushka doll – those nested, hand-painted Russian toy dolls (also known as **matryoshkas**). Nested inside a larger female doll are many inner, progressively smaller girl dolls, with a baby nestled inside them all. I've discovered that **matryoshkas** were inspired by dolls from Japan that are rounded and weighted on the bottom. They're called daruma dolls or **dharma dolls** (see "D is for DIVINE PORPOISE") and are given as good luck "meaning toys" to teach the lesson that things must fall and wobble, but will be righted again. These kinds of dolls are also a metaphor for the design concept of **mise en abîme** or **object within similar object** – as seen in many natural objects, like onions.

The physician-shaman who told me about my babushka dolls didn't know exactly why that part of my soul had fled or what it represented. He said that was for me to decipher. So I endeavored, via shamanic journeying on my own, to find out what part of my life those babushka dolls represented and how I could welcome them back. In my shamanic journey, **lo and behold, they un-nested themselves and became marvelous, tiny dancing babushkas.** A whole row of them danced and pottered about. They told me they were mothering spirits who enjoyed cooking and caring for the family and being nurturers and bustling around the kitchen making wonderful things.

That gave me a big AHA! moment. Maybe I'd left my work in the field of medicine because I longed for time to do other things I'd always wanted to do. For many years, I'd longed to nurture, love, and care for my children, and to make my house a home. That soul fragment probably fled during my medical school residency, when I realized I'd have to forego some of those nurturing and homemaking desires if I was going to survive as a full-time medical resident in training.

It was ironic that the part of my soul that appeared as babushka dolls was retrieved by a fellow physician who was an extremely (hmm, what do I want to say?) masculine male. It felt like the archetype of the masculine male was the very archetype I'd attempted to force myself to align with in order to thrive in the medical field. **In retrieving the nurturing part of me that felt it had to flee in order to survive, I realized that it's a part of me that gives me great joy.**

I'm no Martha Stewart, but I love cooking and creating wonderful food for people. Food has great power, more than many of us want to admit – or maybe just more than I'd wanted to admit. Some of the ancient Vedic texts said that during our time in the world, the time we live in now, the water in the rivers would be bottled up and sold, the food people eat would be cooked at great distances from where it would be eaten, and it would be made without love.

Food made with love is enormously more delicious. Try eating something made with love, by hand, especially for you – even a peanut butter and jelly sandwich you make for yourself – and compare it to something out of a can or frozen and stuck into a box. **When food is made for me with love, including made by me for me with love, I not only enjoy the food more, but feel a deeper sense of nurturance from it.**

In the weeks following that shamanic healing, I discovered a spontaneous renewed interest in cooking healthy, wonderful meals for my family. I reconnected with the joy of concocting wild meals, making them up freestyle from what I found in my refrigerator – a handful of cilantro, couscous, and (why not?) some raisins. Our kids were thrilled that I was more present to nurture them with the food I made (though they weren't totally thrilled with couscous).

That babushka dolls soul retrieval brought back one of my many multitudes, making me larger and more whole. However, I contain many multitudes. There's more.

I've done a lot of wacky stuff in my 45 years on this planet. Looking back, though, it all makes perfect damn sense. For a long time, I had very little insight into why I was the way I was, so my internal road was often lonely, even when I appeared to have many friends. I felt the desire to take a lot of chances, constantly plunging into new and challenging situations, and I was often bewildered.

The more I've accepted and embraced my many multitudes rather than resisting them, the happier I've become. By now, largely because of the born-to-FREAK way I've lived, I've had many epiphanies.

I wonder what it would be like if more people who are born to FREAK (or more parents of kids who are born to FREAK) knew about, loved, and embraced the freeing truth that we contain multitudes. It could change the course of civilization!

We each contain marvelous multitudes. How do we discover our own multitudes and why bother expressing them? Why does claiming our multitudes matter so much? Well, dear reader, **claiming our multitudes is the key to living joyfully and productively.** It's a way of accepting the entirety of who we are.

With the intention of helping *you* uncover your own multitudes, allow me to introduce myself and my multitudes as an example of how our different aspects form and blend to create a whole person.

You'll find stories about my multitudes scattered throughout the book as "Allow Myself to Introduce Myself" chapters.

My dream is that by reading this very bookie you'll get exceedingly curious about your own self. If my dreams come true (and they often do), you will be inspired to discover your own fantastic multitudes. Alice the Elephant and I have some suggestions about exactly how to do that, in the chapter on "Uncover Your Own Multitudes – A Guide."

ELUCIDATING A THROUGH Z

A IS FOR ATTENTION DEFICIT

I am no stranger to mental illness. **I come from an eccentric family of wondrous people who've struggled with depression, anxiety, manic depression, and addiction**. I'm not breaking any confidences when I say that my sister, Maria Bamford, a successful comedian and writer, has struggled mightily. Early on, I sensed that my sister was vulnerable, and I always felt I needed to be tough and strong.

I think I was born with a nice, crusty, protective shell. I was the oldest kid, did well enough in school, and went on to medical school. I wasn't perfect. I was a bit of a risk-taker (doing tequila shots on the first night I had my driver's license) and often bristled at Sunday school authority. **I was grounded for most of high school because I immediately confessed everything I did to my parents**, God bless them. My mother reports that she and my dad prayed a lot when they weren't sighing with anxiety or relief.

A few years back, I was spending my time as a practicing physician (80%), an interior designer (50%), running a website (30%), renovating a house (12%), and raising four kids (100%).

Estimated percentages may vary from the actual. To say my life was "kind of crazy" is like saying Ben and Jerry's Super Fudge Chunk is "kind of good."

Then I heard a few confessions from women who'd recently been diagnosed with Attention Deficit Disorder/Attention Deficit Hyperactive Disorder (ADD/ADHD). It was the diagnosis du jour. I found myself poring over the pages of *Driven to Distraction*, the bestseller about ADD by Harvard physicians John Ratey and Ed Hallowell. **I was blown away. I saw parts of myself on every page. Could it be that I had ADD, too?**

Finally, I went to a well-respected psychologist who took a very thorough history from me and decided that a few attention tests were indicated. He thought it was possible I had ADD and wanted more information.

I thought, modestly (with my post-lunch mocha on board), that I was slaying the Test of Variables of Attention (TOVA), which measures the ability to attend to hideously boring stimulus over time. I was 43, after all. I knew a few things. When I finished at the computer, I looked over and said brightly, "Well, what do you think?" He smiled broadly back at me and said, "Yep, you've definitely got it." **Apparently, I'd performed so poorly on the test that "ADD, Inattentive Type" was a slam-dunk diagnosis.**

Now, I'm not here to debate TOVA or whether or not ADD is even truly a diagnosis. **I want to talk about what an amazing gift it was to receive the diagnosis and to have a label for how I am.**

I went home and immediately read approximately 54 tomes on the topic of ADD (they say the way you do one thing is the way you do everything). Of course, I skimmed the parts I didn't find interesting. But this time, **as I skimmed – something I'd done** forever – I laughed. Hello! I have ADD and THAT'S WHAT WE DO. We skim.

> Some labels hurt, like too
> sensitive, too intense,
> too much, too loud.
> Find new ones,
> like aahhhmazing,
> fantastic, big life lover!
>
> " *Alice*

Then I cried. I cried for little Sarah, who'd been too much, too loud, too insatiable, who'd had too many questions, too many ideas, too much energy. I cried for young-adult Sarah, who spent the first two years of college at the library studying in complete isolation in order to get the grades she needed to get into medical school. I cried for the exhausted mother of four little kids, who'd worked full-time and had a spouse who was also a physician devoted to his craft. **But something had shifted.** What I'd always suspected – that I was different – had been confirmed.

Attention Deficit **is truly the worst possible name for this condition.** We don't lack attention so much as use it differently. We have the superpower of hyper-focus – what I like to call *hocus-pocus* **focus** (more about that in "H is for HOCUS-POCUS FOCUS"). Most of the time, those of us with ADD are in a state of wide-open focus, **taking in everything all at once.** That's when we may appear to be "spacey" or as if we're somewhere else. When something captures our attention, though, look out! **We have the ability to lock in through the magic of hocus-pocus focus.**

When I found out I had ADD, I got busy. **I used my hyper-focusing abilities – the gift of ADD that makes me like a dog with a bone.** I hired an ADD Coach and, through my physician, began trying out low doses of medication to see if it helped. The first day, I took a small test dose and picked up a really boring book. I turned to a really boring topic and sat there quietly reading the entire passage word by word for a long time. It was weird. I didn't look up. I didn't think about Tina Fey or the peonies in my garden or making salsa from scratch … I just read. Apparently, my brain on ADD meds is like the brain of a normal person (if there even is a "normal").

I talked to everyone I knew who'd been diagnosed with ADD to see what I could glean from their experiences. Some of the stuff I had read was disheartening, yet as I looked for and found and talked with others with ADD, **I discovered so many amazing people with ADD who were creative, productive, and living well.** That gave me hope … but I still wanted to know how to stop feeling overwhelmed.

I began to navigate the world differently, **newly aware of my unique ability to hyper-focus on things I love and tune out anything I'm not interested in or consider boring.** Think about that for a minute. How lucky was I to be able to do that?

I also realized why it was challenging for me to keep a Google calendar with six different schedules updated. I forgave myself for wigging out completely whenever a new sport commenced for one of my kids, with its barrage of detail-filled emails, practice schedules, and endless phone calls about carpooling, all of which pushed me over the edge. Other parents seemed completely nonplussed about it, but **I had hard data from the professionals showing that I didn't do well with work I hated** – like filing taxes, keeping track of other people's schedules, and remembering mind-numbing details like dental appointment dates.

People started showing up in my life to reassure me about how okay it all was. Martha Beck and her lovely tribe of coaches cackled and giggled during a phone call I was on to discuss the possibility of going through Martha's coach training. They joked about how likely it was that they all had ADD. Martha said something like, "Oh, yeah. I have the attention span of a squirrel!" I thought, GOOD GAWWWD??! You mean somebody thinks this is funny, absolutely no big deal, and even speaks of it in public?! Learning from that tribe how to be transparent, authentic, and open helped me enormously. I was learning that it was okay to be me and, in fact, I might get demerits if I was NOT!

Next, unbelievably bright and shining lights, like Jeannette Maw, founder of Good Vibe University, showed up to help me reclaim my own beauty. **With Jeannette, not only was it okay to act like you'd "just snorted rocket fuel," it was celebrated.** That's what people came to Jeannette for – to witness her in that place of complete blast-off. And I was one of them. I know what it feels like to be that enthusiastic, to be that "high on life." In many ways, **that's what ADD gives us – glimpses of ecstasy and cosmic connection** (and, potentially, their polar opposites, of course). Through all of this, I was developing more and more compassion for myself and others.

Since then, through my personal work and my work with clients and groups, I've made so many connections between ADD, high sensitivity, Asperger's syndrome, autism, addicts of every kind (sex, drugs, alcohol, gambling, shopping), depressed/anxious people, intense people, change agents, black sheep, adrenaline junkies, irrepressibles, rebels, bohemians, life pirates, bad asses, artists, innovators, performers, comedians, and healers ... and I believe we were all born to FREAK. **We were all put here not to fit in, but to see things differently, to ruffle feathers, and to**

return balance to the world and our communities by using our creative abilities, our healing presence, and our eccentric gifts.

I decided to take a six-month sabbatical from my medical practice to focus on my coaching practice and on myself. During that time, **I found deep reassurance and healing in the woods.** I stumbled onto the practice of shamanism, which, to me, seems uniquely positioned in this time as an extremely accessible, low-cost way for humans to become empowered and to seek healing for the spiritual aspects of disease.

S*HAMANISM is actually a way of life. Its main tenet is that everything that is, is alive. A shaman is an intermediary between the world of spirits and the more solid-appearing world of form. Shamans undertake journeys to the spirit worlds (via soul flight) to ask for healing on behalf of themselves or others or to bring a community back into balance. Taking a shamanic journey via drumming causes the brain to enter a theta wave state, where brain waves are at the frequency of dreaming or REM sleep. Perhaps not coincidentally, some EEG studies of the brains of some people with ADD (the "daydreamy types") show that theta brain waves predominate. Those of us who were born to FREAK may be uniquely positioned to conduct the ancient work of shamanism.*

Shamanism views a mental health crisis as an initiation. Traditionally, if the village shaman offered healing and the stricken person had a desire to heal, that once-weakened

person would be healed and become more powerful, raised up to a higher level of performance. I like that idea.

So if you've just received some sort of mental health diagnosis (or are close to someone who has), **consider the exciting and**

amazing possibility that you (or they) are being prepared for something greater. I don't say this to belittle the struggle or the difficulty and pain of depression, ADHD, bipolar/manic depression, anxiety, borderline personality disorder, or any of the other diagnoses, but to offer hope. **There is always hope.**

Eventually, on one of my shamanic journeys, I asked for a healing from my ADD. I wasn't sure what was supposed to happen, but I knew I was ready to go to another level with it. Days later, several things happened that resulted in a convergence of feeling empowered, including laughing hysterically for a weekend with friends about my ADD. I realized that I belong. I also realized that the more I revel in my Sarah-ness, my ADD-ness, the better off we all are. The next week, on Good Vibe University, I launched a call on this topic that was very well received and that became the impetus for writing this book.

I have preposterously fantastic ADD skills and I am no longer afraid to use them.

I'm becoming quite enamored with my own muchness. What excites me most is seeing people fall in love with their own muchness. The world needs us. And it's later than you think (wink), so let's get a move on.

✾✾ In what way were you born to FREAK?

✾✾ What does your MUCHNESS look like?

✾✾ What do you do that draws people, like moths to a flame?

Allow Myself to Introduce Myself

SCHOLAR OF MYSELF

SCHOLAR OF MYSELF

My high school guidance counselor, with whom I had a single meeting, clearly didn't know me at all. He strongly suggested I go to a Catholic women's college instead of to Kenyon, but my **anthropological study of Catholic natives was over.** I'd already "been there, done that" during high school. I knew myself. I was ready to expand my research and move on to something bigger and wilder.

On my exploratory visit to Kenyon College in rural Ohio, I noticed a fair number of what seemed like exciting individuals from all over the country. Plus, it was a gorgeous campus, fulfilling my need for aesthetics. I liked it! It was going to be an adventure!

By the time I selected a college, I'd already been a scholar of myself for quite a while. If you were to read the little book I kept under my bed between the ages of six and sixteen, you'd see my carefully chronicled aspirations throughout that time period.

In the early years, I wanted to be a veterinarian's assistant (alas! impossible, as I was terrified of dogs). Later, I wanted to be a veterinarian's nurse. I'd read the entire series of 50s-era novels about Cherry Ames, a mystery-solving nurse. She made nursing sound like a romantic and highly awesome occupation. **She often had to take the heat from supervisors after she'd followed her intuition and broken the rules, but she always came out on top!** (Obviously, Cherry was born to FREAK). Eventually, from around age twelve on, the book under my bed listed "doctor" as my occupation of choice.

Why a doctor? Well, I suppose society, as well as family influences, had gotten to me by then. I did sincerely want to help people, but, at the same time, after watching my mother kowtow to my father, I also wanted to experience world domination (or the closest thing to it), which meant being like my father, who was a doctor. I'm a fourth-generation physician. Was being a doctor in my genetic code?

Interestingly, by the time I went to college, the book under my bed noted my career aspirations as "chef, doctor, or news reporter." Though I knew **I didn't naturally have the anchor hair I'd need to be on TV (glossy, freely swinging hair unaffected by hail or moisture)**, I figured wigs were getting better, so there was hope for a career as a reporter. Cooking was a lifelong love of mine, and being a chef appeared to be a way to cook as a career. I think what was going on was that as I got closer to actually having a career, I became scared I might not get into medical school, so I hedged my bets.

I headed off to Kenyon College and discovered that even though the subject matter I had to study to get into medical school was stuff I probably had some natural ability in, it did not particularly thrill me. In my heart, I'd always really loved reading and dreamed that somehow, maybe, I could also write. I think that was only a semi-conscious dream, as I failed to note it in my under-the-bed book of aspirations. Being an author may have seemed too foreign to be a real possibility. There were no writer role models around.

English was one of the subjects I expected to enjoy the most (that writer aspiration trying to creep in!), but it dealt me some harsh blows. By "harsh blows" I mean that I got a B+ on my first English paper. Naturally, I figured that meant I wasn't cut out to be a writer. If I was, I would've gotten an A or an A+.

sarah bamford seidelmann m.d. | www.borntoFREAK.com

Why do we allow our dreams to be dashed so easily? What made me so vulnerable to disappointment? I suppose it was the same thing that makes me vulnerable to so much joy and enthusiasm: I had high hopes!

So, with English major (and then journalist) scratched off my list, and with no culinary classes in sight, college became all about pre-med. I was excited even while I was unsure. I felt a lot of pressure. I felt like I had to earn all As. So I arose at dawn and lived in the library, **surviving on small satchels of corn bran cereal** (which my loving mother mailed to me until they became available in the college feeding troughs), adding tiny chocolate chips for a measure of joy.

Pre-med eventually led to medical school, residency, and a flourishing career in pathology. My life sailed smoothly ahead for a long time, and my self-study went on hiatus.

More than a dozen years later, when things got confusing and I was really not having fun at work or at home, **I started asking myself questions again.** I began again to record my likes, aspirations, and dreams, this time in notebooks I left scattered around the house. I made notes about my Myers-Briggs testing results and about possibilities. I considered my love of homes and design and style. Did I want to be an interior designer? I noted my reading tastes, which leaned heavily toward self-help, spirituality, inspiration, and human potential.

I'd always enjoyed being a scholar of myself, and I knew how to do it, even though I'd taken a break from it for a while. I asked myself what I'd done previously that had worked, what had made me happy, and what I liked doing. What were my strengths? What was I best suited for? What did I long for? I reviewed and observed my failures and successes and tried to understand why they'd happened. I noticed the kinds of people I blossomed around and the kinds of environments that made me feel stifled. And I recorded it all.

The clues to what we adore are there when we look back at ourselves as children. It's rawwwther fascinating that when I left medicine I sort of returned to my roots of wanting to be a veterinarian's assistant, in that I now often work with humans in a way that involves the study and observation of animals as totems. I love it that this work serves both humans and animals.

Being a scholar of myself has shown me the key ingredients required to create a life that's perfectly suited to me: I'm a writer; I get to play chef (to the people I love most); I get to be a healer (sometimes teaching others how to keep their own under-the-bed notebooks); and I occasionally get to take center stage, like a TV news presenter.

IS FOR

BLACK MAMBA

I've realized that power scares the bejesus out of most of us humans ... or, wait, is it just me?

If we had real power, what would be asked of us? No, no, I don't want power. Just give me some money, a beach house, a subscription to the Oprah Winfrey Network, and a few J. Crew cashmere sweaters in the Pantone color of the year and I'll be okay. **Being loaded up with pure, raw, unadulterated, universe-bending, actual power?** Sheesh, no, you can keep that. That might be too horrifyingly troublesome.

> Step into your elephant power.
> This kind of power is not granted,
> but taken. Seize it.
>
> " *Alice*

Why do we shirk or give away **our universe-granted right to create our own lives,** to form, shape, and heal the world, to please ourselves?

Are you asking me?

Well, I don't know about you, but I've found it much, much easier to sit back and complain, to cuss out the people in charge (the boss, the administration, the world, God, my mother, my husband's mother) than to take back my own power. Good girls are not full of power, in the superhero, shamanic, or universe-bending way. **To be full of power, I'd have to surrender my Official Good-Girl Card.**

I learned about being full of power from a BLACK MAMBA snake.

Like power, snakes (especially venomous ones) scare the heck out of most normal humans. As they should. Such snakes can kill you, eat you for breakfast, then slither off without bothering to have another thought except, **wow, that was delish!**

The snake that educated me was an archetypal (thank God) BLACK MAMBA that came to me in a dream, carved and lifeless on a wooden sign. No big whoop. Later, I realized she was wrapped around a stick all caduceus-like. A carved BLACK MAMBA might seem like nothing major, but it still scared me so much I immediately exited the dream and woke up.

T HE CADUCEUS SYMBOL *is two serpents wrapped around a stick with wings on the top. People in the U.S. often recognize this as the sign of medicine, but originally the caduceus was a symbol of commerce. The Rod of Asclepius (one serpent and a stick with no wings at the top) was associated with medicine and healing. Apparently, over years of miscommunication and misdocumentation, the caduceus became associated with the medical profession in the U.S. As a symbol for commerce, the two serpents of the caduceus originally symbolized balance and reciprocity.*

sarah bamford seidelmann m.d. | www.borntoFREAK.com

Most scary dreams have wonderful messages for us, but we FREAK out and leave too soon to receive them. After I had that BLACK MAMBA dream, I remembered that before I'd gone to sleep I'd asked for a helpful animal or Beastie to show itself. So I decided to revisit the mamba ... but before our rematch I watched a lot of BBC footage of BLACK MAMBAS. I took note of their elegance (especially while swimming through water, lifting their head and part of their body into the air), their beauty, and their frighteningly powerful venom. **Sometimes, studying the stuff that scares the bejesus out of us helps a lot.**

I used a technique of shamanic journeying to re-enter my dream with the mamba. Inside the dream, I asked her what she wanted with me. She indicated that she simply wanted me to dance with her. I refused. I'd hoped she'd just tell me something juicy so I could get out fast. I was embarrassed about the idea of dancing with her and didn't understand the purpose of it. **I just wanted to learn something. Why did I have to DO anything?**

In a nonchalant way, the BLACK MAMBA threatened me, telling me that if I didn't dance with her, she'd bite me. Wow. Really? Come on, let's stay peaceful here. Though I didn't want to be bitten, I stubbornly refused to dance. So ... **the BLACK MAMBA bit me, as promised.** That really scared me. At the time, I was lying on the floor of my walk-in closet, underneath the hanging J. Crew sweaters and bohemian wear, amongst many baskets of black velour lounge pants. (It was the only place in my house I could find to take an undisturbed shamanic journey.)

After she bit me, I thought, **Oh, my God. This is how it's going to go down. I've been bitten by a BLACK MAMBA snake in my closet and will now die here alone.** That's how terrifyingly real it felt. Thankfully, I had my Core Beastie with me. When I looked in panic at my Core Beastie, she seemed entirely casual about the whole thing, as if to say, **Go on and take your whoopin' so we can go home.**

CORE BEASTIES *What some people call power animals I call* Core Beasties, *a term I thought up because, for me, it better communicates what these relationships are about. A Core Beastie is an animal you have a relationship with over a very long period of time, even over a lifetime. A connection with a Core Beastie is empowering, but not in the way our culture tends to think of using power – to dominate the world or control others. The Beastie kind of empowerment is the quiet strength that comes from being and expressing your unique essence in all realms of your life. An empowering relationship with a Core Beastie can be one of the most magical friendships and mentorships you'll ever have. That's what it's been for me. (For more about connecting with Beasties and Core Beasties, see my first book,* What the Walrus Knows.*)*

In my closet, that shamanic journey ended when I took my whooping. After I'd returned to the closet floor, I looked at that journey from an archetypal viewpoint and saw something new. How many times in my life had I been asked to step up, but refused or been so terrified that I tried to avoid it any way I could? Let's review ...

1 At YMCA camp in 1976, I refused to ride horses, citing a letter my mother had written forbidding me to ride (she knew I was scared), yet after my cabin counselor talked me into it, I ended up loving it.

2 I refused to be the MC at my a cappella group's concert at Kenyon College because after the rave reviews I got for my first MC job I had a fear of failing to do it well a second time.

After the tsunami-like emotions I felt and had no idea how to handle while being with patients in medical school, I refused to do direct patient care. I chose pathology instead.

 And so many other times when I rebelled or pretended I didn't care about things and stood on the sidelines rather than stepping up and participating.

Realizing all of this, I also realized I was sick and tired of not standing up to my fears, to the BLACK MAMBAS in my life. So I gathered all my courage and lay back down on my closet floor to revisit that BLACK MAMBA yet again.

> To keep your ego in check,
> do stuff that challenges you.
> Humility must be fostered.
>
> " *Alice*

This time, it was different. I surrendered. I was scared, mind you, but I still surrendered. I took my Core Beastie along, of course (thank God I never have to be alone on these EPIC life journeys).

BLACK MAMBA had us follow her out to a huge field, like the plains of Mongolia – breathtakingly beautiful, wild, and open. Once there, she indicated it was time to dance. So we began. My Core Beastie (a bear) and I danced back and forth, trying to imitate the BLACK MAMBA's movements. At first, it was awkward trying to dance like a snake. **It's not easy to mamba, people**. As we danced, my logical mind was full of **What's the point of all this? I don't understand why I'm doing this? Why is this happening?** ... and then I had a wordless experience. I became filled with a peaceful, powerful energy that caused me to grow and grow and grow until I billowed over the mamba and my Core Beastie, like a Macy's Thanksgiving Day Parade inflatable.

I wasn't sure what had happened, but when I returned from that journey, I knew I'd experienced power.

It turns out that real, honest-to-goodness power isn't scary or terrifying. It feels like a peaceful knowing. **Real power feels like being utterly supported and empowered by the universe. It actually feels totally fantastic.** So why do we avoid it? Because the process of owning our power can be terrifying.

As terrifying as it may be to accept your power, it's there for the taking, whenever you decide you're ready.

 What's the first thing you'd do if you had a boatload of true power?

IS FOR

CHANGE AGENT

We who were born to FREAK are always, incessantly, asking "*Why?*," challenging authority, and questioning the status quo. Non-FREAKS have told me it's exhausting to watch. But it's how our FREAKY brains work best. **We smell injustice, we hear the tiniest voice of frustration within a conversation, and we notice change in the wind.** We can't help it.

No matter what I'm doing, **my injustice radar is always on alert.** In our spiffy new food co-op, I notice how wonderful things are ("This feels good!"), and then ("Oh dear ...") I notice that some of the water they carry was bottled in Europe, then shipped (no doubt on horrifying, exhaust-belching ocean liners for days on end, then on big trucks, all burning up thousands of gallons of fuel) to our small Midwestern city for our drinking enjoyment. Huh? This flies in the face of everything I thought we (the co-op) stood for!? I quickly switch from appreciation (feeling good) to haughty disapprobation (feeling not so good).

I sniff out strife everywhere. In the contents of my seven-year-old's backpack I found a colorful card with balloons on it that said "Charlie is 100 days smarter today." What the heck does that mean? Then I get all existential about it. Is he a hundred days smarter now or was he smarter a hundred days before you teachers started trying to mold his beautiful, precious, innocent mind? Or, worse yet, is he 2555 days less smart since my husband and I took charge of his life on the planet? And what do they mean by smart anyway? On and on. My brain oozes possibilities, weighing and assessing everything.

Sure, it can be torture some days to question everything. But **critical evaluation is part of being a FREAK. We always want to know where we stand.** We're always wondering if things could be better and, if so, how? We want to know what's beneath all the hustle and flow. What's really going on? As fascinating as it all is, it can be exhausting.

The loosier and goosier, the better.

" *Alice*

The key, for me, has been to stay buoyant, to be loose like a goose and float on top of it all. I've gathered many ways to move through life without getting lost in details and dead ends. For example, I use the Serenity Prayer.

T**HE SERENITY PRAYER** *"God, grant me the serenity to accept the things I cannot change, the courage to change the things I can, and the wisdom to know the difference." – Reinhold Niebuhr*

Also, **I imagine that every area of potential change represents a door inside the beautiful Taj Mahal** (see "L is for LOVE"). There's not remotely enough time to explore every single door (in this life, anyhoo). So I try to choose the doors that are most beautiful – the doors I care deeply about and am really drawn to.

> When there are a thousand
> doors to choose from, walk through
> the one that feels like love.
>
> " *Alice*

At this point in my life, I'm focused on facilitating healing for other humans. I love to encourage people to seek guidance about getting on their own best path. When I remember that *that* is one of the most beautiful doors in my personal Taj Mahal, it's easier not to get caught up in trying to seize power at the co-op or steamroll the PTA board into stopping teachers from giving out those "100-days-smarter" awards.

> To hell with what everybody else is up to.
> Sheeeesh! The question, my dear human,
> is what are YOU creating? Hope it's
> amazeballs. Cheerio.
>
> " *Alice*

We FREAKS are shit-stirrers and troublemakers, intense agitators who won't be ignored. We will change the world. It's our destiny.

But you can't do it all ... well, you could try, but that could lead to failure (see "F is for FAIL") and overall exhaustion. They key is knowing what part of the world you want to change. What part do you want to play? **What kind of impact on the world would feel good to you?** Choose the most gorgeous door, the one that matters the most to you. **Choose what feels like love. Then you can't go wrong.**

Commit to very little.
Drill down to three projects.
(Then surrender to the fact
that you WILL deviate.)
" *Alice*

If, once you open that door, you end up not liking what's behind it ... go back and try a different door. It may be hard to predict where a door will take you, but if you like the looks of it, go ahead and walk through, into the beautiful mystery, and find out.

 As a born-to-FREAK CHANGE AGENT who sniffs out ways the world could be better, which few of all the beautiful doors facing you in your personal Taj Mahal most beguile you?

Allow Myself to Introduce Myself

PIONEER WOMAN

PIONEER WOMAN

I was named after Sarah Townsend, an ancestor on my mother's side. When I was in third grade, my mother overheard me explain my unusual middle name to a friend. "I was named after a millionaire in Iowa," I told my friend emphatically. From the other room, my mother shouted out, **"*Pioneer*, honey, not millionaire. PIONEER! You were named for a pioneer woman."** I heard her sigh heavily.

Those pesky damn details again. I'm not sure if I made up *millionaire* because it sounded more exciting (likely!) or whether it was just that the words sounded a bit similar. *Pioneer* was a tough concept to wrap my mind around, but *millionaire* made sense after watching *Dallas* on TV.

Well, I hear the names we give our children are often prophetic.

During my medical residency in pathology, I knew that in order to define myself as a unique asset, I would need to stand apart. That meant I needed to subspecialize. Yet none of the local, existing residency subfellowships appealed to me. I loved the role of dermatopathologist, a specialist in skin diseases, but knew that with a new baby I didn't want to leave town or live apart from my husband for a year. So, true to my born-to-FREAK nature, I created my own local version of a dermatopathology fellowship, with the aid of my born-to-FREAK advisor.

Many people I worked with during that fellowship had questions or doubted what I was up to. I also questioned myself. Without an official subspecialty fellowship, would I ever get a

sarah bamford seidelmann m.d. | www.borntoFREAK.com

job? Following my own previously unpaved trail confused some of the residents and doctors I worked with that year. One doctor in private practice was so upset he confronted me about it. **He seemed to think I had a secret plot to steal all his work!** It wasn't easy to be a residency fellowship pioneer – I had to develop a thick skin.

> Never hold back. Be you.
> You were born to ruffle feathers.
>
> " *Alice*

Even though it caused a ruckus, creating my own fellowship turned out to be one of the best moves I made. As I'd suspected, almost no one in private practice enjoyed analyzing skin biopsies, which I loved doing, so my subspecialty turned out to be in demand.

The wacky pioneering and pirate-like characters of my medical training days at various hospitals seemed to exit stage left when I entered a smaller city group private practice. It was a bit like joining a partially loving but also somewhat dysfunctional family. I felt stifled. Out in the real world, my joyful, pioneering nature, which had been welcomed in the innovative academic arena, was initially met with concern or, worse yet, disdain. I was the "new lady pathologist" in town and, as such, was expected to prove myself before I'd be accepted.

My first day at work in private practice required me to call upon my inner pioneer. A surgeon requested a particular procedure which, in my opinion, would cause problems for accurate diagnosis. I tried to communicate this to the surgeon through a technician, but the surgeon sent back word that she wanted what she'd originally asked for. She was used to having it done that way.

After I hung up the phone, I sat there stunned for a minute. The technician had advised me not to get into a confrontation with that surgeon, as she could be quite formidable. Apparently, no one gave her no for an answer. I didn't relish combat with an established surgeon on day one, yet knew I'd been trained in state-of-the-art procedures and didn't want to compromise the patient's care.

I called the operating room directly over the intercom and attempted to tell the surgeon why I didn't want to do the procedure as requested, preferring to do it a better way instead. The surgeon's response was to march into the lab where I worked. I explained my reasoning. Though she wasn't too happy, she stopped arguing and we did it my way, which benefited the patient.

My partners expressed shock that I'd refused to do something the surgeon had asked me to, as she was considered a very important client and colleague. When I explained my reasoning to my partners, supporting it with the professional articles I'd read, they seemed to calm down. Soon afterwards, all the partners I worked with started doing the procedure the new way. It was the right thing to do. It was the new standard of care.

Nope. Pioneering is not for the meek of heart.

After a couple of years, I was more than ready to move on from the somewhat stifling environment of my first practice and get back into a bigger game. I entered a practice that was totally

sarah bamford seidelmann m.d. | www.borntoFREAK.com

stimulating, at a very large medical center that served a huge geographic area. My partners were all so smart and wise and generous in teaching me what they knew. I thrived, enjoying the new challenges laid before me.

I was immediately given the responsibility of overhauling a department in need of change, and I really enjoyed that challenge. I saw how things could be better and enlisted talented people to help me implement the changes. Some of those changes were very difficult and terribly unpopular, but that department eventually became a real source of pride for all of us.

I love it when my pioneering ways are welcomed. Being the instigator of change, the first person to do something or to do something in a unique way, can be daunting and intimidating and bring up a lot of internal questions. **When I pioneer, I check in with my heart of hearts.** If what I'm doing excites me and feels good, I trust and carry on, because I know I'm going where I want to go.

Be positively addicted to the new.
New spiritual ideas, new ways to
be healthy, new ways to play.

Reinvent, upgrade, and expand daily.

" *Alice*

D IS FOR

DIVINE PORPOISE

Dharma is a wild and wooly ancient Sanskrit word with numerous layers of meaning. I'm not suggesting you go look it up in Wikipedia and study its layered wooliness – unless you're feeling thorough and detail-oriented. (I wasn't, it turns out.) To me, dharma is simply the idea that **when we align with our DIVINE PORPOISE/purpose (our purposeful porpoise), we can swim merrily through life's oceans with abundance and ease.**

Allow goodness to flow through you.
Become a clear channel.

 Alice

I first discovered the concept of dharma a decade or so ago, listening to the lulling and funky vocal stylings of Deepak Chopra in his audiobook *The Seven Spiritual Laws of Success*. Because of my mental exhaustion (I was raising babies and working as a physician full-time), I could barely make out what he was talking about in most of the recordings. His accent was pretty crazy, but then so was I. Oddly, the dharma thing sunk in. Now I see that Deeps endorses everything from yoga DVDs and Xbox games to supplements with names like Endorphinate. **It turns out Deeps was born to FREAK and has a lot of DIVINE PORPOISES.**

This idea that there's a divinity in me that, if harnessed properly, can lead me to live a great life and be in bliss – **Well**, I thought, **what could be better than that? I'll take a platter of dharma with a side of bliss.** The only trouble was that I didn't have a damn clue what was divine in me.

Something I've learned about those who were born to FREAK is that we often have a poor sense of ourselves. Perhaps it's because we have the ability to be really porous (not unlike Sponge Bob), merging with the universe until we have trouble seeing who we really are. I've learned that it's very good to know what our own gifts are so we can **get down with our DIVINE PORPOISE.**

Many things have helped me figure myself out. **Knowing thyself is fucking powerful** – it can clear a lot of confusion out of the way and unlock a lot of doors. It's also a bit of a process. Sometimes messy. (Bring extra napkins.)

There are so many ways to discover what your gifts are, but perhaps none so powerful as simply asking the people who love you. Yes, actually ask other people 1) what they experience when they're with you, and 2) what they think your strengths and gifts are. **Being born to FREAK, we may have previously gotten quite a bit of negative feedback.** We may have a poor sense of ourselves as a separate individual and find it difficult to see who we really are.

ASKING FRIENDS ABOUT YOUR GIFTS *Do NOT, under any circumstances, ask them about your WORST qualities. Yes, you have these, too, but, good Gawwwd, don't focus on them!*

Years ago, when I asked some good friends to tell me how they felt around me and what they saw in me, **I was baffled by their responses.** One person said, "Wow! You're brave to ask." I suppose so. But what a gift I got in return!

People said I was a good listener (Whaaaat?? I thought I talked too much and interrupted way too much). **People said they felt uplifted around me, as though anything was possible** (Really? I often felt like I was a downer.) They said that being around me made them feel like doing something, that when they were around me they were somehow goaded into action. All of that surprised me. Slowly, I was able to recognize that I actually had some of those wonderful qualities.

Living your DIVINE PORPOISE requires that you know and embrace what you have within that's divine, and that you harness and share it.

> Go for broke. Dream in absurd
> and ridiculous directions.
> That's where the magic is, dagnabbit!
> Then take little feel-good
> steps towards the magic.
>
> " *Alice*

Here's an incomplete list of other things I've done over the years to dig up my dharma and identify my DIVINE PORPOISE: Myers Briggs testing, visualization, VIA inventory of strengths (viacharacter.org), StrengthsFinder 2.0, Conative Style Testing (Kolbe.com), forest bathing (see my book *What the Walrus Knows*), shamanic work, coaching, and looking back at things I did that went very well. Any of those can be fantastic tools, and I recommend them all.

Each of us has within a marvelous soup, a divine concoction of qualities that's so unique it's never been seen in the universe and never will be again (see "Our Multitudes"). The way I look at it, it's our job to express our combination of qualities in the most beautiful ways we can. **Sing and strum them, paint and write them, dance them, parkour them, surf them, film them, cook and sashay them out into the world.**

Do your best work. Love why you do it.
The results are out of our trunks
(or your hands).

" *Alice*

Whenever we express our own divine inner consommé, we enter a beautiful place where time is nonexistent **(unless someone is rudely trying to call you back from your DIVINE PORPOISE experience to make tacos for dinner, as sometimes happens to me).** Expressing my DIVINE PORPOISE often happens in the hyper-focused state of ADD. I get so captivated by writing or creating a video or examining images that hours pass by but I feel like it was only two minutes. **What's that? Wait. Someone's shouting off in the distance.** Oh, it's one of my kids. Ack! What? I only have five minutes to change out of these black velour lounge pants, brush my teeth, and take you to the dentist?!

I have a humungous painting of the Hindu deity Lakshmi in my house, which I bought years ago because I loved it. At the time I bought it, I had no idea that it's a depiction of dharma in action. Lakshmi is seated on a lotus with an elephant on either side gently spraying her with water from above. **Lakshmi is a metaphorical image of DIVINE PORPOISE.** As she sits in meditation, golden nectar spills from her hands out into the world.

A version of Lakshmi's experience is what I've come to know as the feeling of living my own DIVINE PORPOISE: I'm seated in bliss with a perfect, never-ending source of delicate, patient elephant rain splashing down over me. From this blissful state, goodness and nectar flow outward from me into the world.

Yes, some days I do feel more like I fell off the lotus into the mud. It happens. It'll happen to you, too. That's okay. Just climb back up onto the lotus and ride on. When you live your DIVINE PORPOISE, cleansing, healing elephant rain is always available to you.

 What do you do that comes easily and takes you into a state of bliss (like elephant rain)?

 What appeals to you as a way to learn more about your DIVINE PORPOISE?

Do what you're fucking amazing at.

" *Alice*

Allow Myself to
Introduce Myself

TENDER
OF SOULS

TENDER OF SOULS

As my medical school classmates and I began our rotations in clinical areas like surgery, internal medicine, and neurology, I began thinking about what kind of doctor I wanted to be. A few experiences I had as I navigated the practice of medicine shaped my choices and eventually led me to embrace myself as a tender of souls.

During a rotation in internal medicine at a prestigious private hospital known for its academically oriented physicians, I worked on the oncology floor, where they used the newest treatment for late-stage breast cancer: a bone marrow transplant that was very hard on the patients. Those treatments were eventually stopped because they killed more people than they helped. Witnessing the brutality of those treatments and not knowing how to comfort the patients (or myself) was excruciating.

I vividly remember a 29-year-old patient, a recently divorced woman with three young children, who'd had a bone marrow transplant for advanced breast cancer. Her blood platelets had dipped dangerously low, despite innumerable transfusions. We waited anxiously for her bone marrow to recover and start making its own platelets. As I stood at her bedside, I felt so unhelpful, so positively bewildered. I wanted to deal with what was going on in her head and her heart, but I didn't know how. I wanted to comfort her, to make her hardships go away so she could go home and be with her three little kids. I couldn't articulate it then, but **I yearned to address the needs of her soul.**

The next day, while in an echo-filled stairwell at the hospital, we got a page informing us that the bone marrow transplant patient had bled to death that morning. Her body had given up the fight. We sat down on the cement stairs and allowed ourselves a little

sarah bamford seidelmann m.d. | www.borntoFREAK.com

weep. No opening of the floodgates – we had very little time for feeling feelings; there was too much to do. **Just a small recognition that we were human beings who felt at a loss.**

Although I felt a need to address and change similar struggles and experiences so many other patients were going through, I came to the conclusion that I wasn't prepared or equipped to do such a thing. I figured I'd need some kind of special therapy training to become the kind of healer I felt I wanted to be, and I didn't have a clue where to begin.

After another, similar experience, during a rotation on the organ transplant unit, I was left feeling terribly unsure about the field of medicine. **It all seemed so barbaric. No one seemed to address matters of the human spirit.** My fellow students seemed unphased by those issues, or, if they were affected by them, they didn't speak of it. I told myself I didn't have the luxury of time (or so I thought) to fix whatever the hell was broken in me, so I kept pushing onward.

My next rotation was with a merry, motley band of brilliant, pirate-like individuals who ran the department of pathology. I witnessed much excitement during that rotation. We'd be in the frozen section room (where tissue is rapidly diagnosed during a surgery) and one of the pathologists would push the button on the "squawk box" (as we called the intercom) and shout to the surgeon in the operating room, "Get the fuck down here! [pirate pathologist–speak for "All hands on deck!"] I have a doozy of a cranial thing. Bring the others, too."

Pathology was thrilling and challenging – no tumor or patient or case was exactly the same. The pathologists I worked with were brilliant, quirky, hilarious, and deeply in love with their work. I was hooked.

It didn't hurt that pathology is a mostly visual sport, and I have innate visual and pattern-recognition abilities. I'd spent my life studying patterns – in the woods, on wallpaper, in all things beautiful. I decided that in finding pathology, I'd found something I truly loved. I'd also found a way to avoid dealing directly with patients. **By becoming a pathologist, I temporarily dodged my calling of being a tender of souls.**

After working a few years in a pathology practice, I started paying attention again to what was happening in the patient arena. As I sat in a breast cancer conference and listened to stories of patients dealing with abusive spouses, struggling with body image and sexuality issues, and lacking helpful relatives and friends, I again felt that familiar sense of discontent growing within me. I noticed that those kinds of patient issues were usually brought up by social workers and nurse practitioners rather than doctors. The doctors seemed to brush those patient issues off as unimportant. "We're here to talk about cancer, chemo, and radiation," they'd say. But it felt to me that no matter what kind of EPIC chemo we were talking about dosing out, we'd be doing the patient a disservice if they had to go through it alone and bewildered.

Around that time, the painful realization that the kind of medicine we were practicing didn't serve patients at a soul level resurfaced for me. **I finally gave myself the opportunity to explore what soul-centered healing would look like** and took a six-month sabbatical. During those six months, I realized that tending souls is all I'd ever wanted to do in the first place.

Now I've returned to the soul-tending work I believe I've been called to do all my life. **The soul is our vital essence.** It's the nonphysical, or spirited, part of us. Through my coaching and shamanic work, **I address all of the issues of the soul that I'd**

sarah bamford seidelmann m.d. | www.borntoFREAK.com

longed to address during all those many, frustrated years I spent training to be a doctor and working as a doctor. When I do soul work on behalf of others, time stops and I feel like I'm doing exactly what I am meant to be doing.

IS FOR

EPIC

A lovely friend and fellow FREAK once said to me, "It kind of scares me when you say the word EPIC so much." Well, I suppose it should. **Though I'm no longer scared about it, I do take my EPIC seriously.** When I say, for example, "The surfing in Hawaii will be EPIC," it means I'll be surrounded by like-minded nine- to 59-year-olds in about four feet of water and **my compadres will be shouting to me, "Explore the space!" as I ride an approximately seven-inch wave gloriously towards shore.**

How do we describe the indescribable, the powerfully ineffable? *EPIC* works for me. *EPIC* feels majestic and heroic.

I like the word *EPIC* because it goads (see "G is for GOADING"). When I feel like calling something **EPIC**, I'm forced to ask myself questions like these:

 Is this [project, trip, event, idea] worthy of my heroic journey?

 Does it feel EPIC enough to be worthy of my energy?

Is it a great achievement?

4 How could this achievement be greater?

When you're creating at the EPIC or mythic level, you may be very afraid. Though you're naturally powerful beyond measure, you may not be used to living in that power (see "B is for BLACK MAMBA"). It can be particularly powerful to take problems or tough issues to the EPIC level, to a mythical place of power that's beyond or beneath or before this conundrum or mess or whatever's bothering us.

From the shamanic viewpoint, everything you see or experience in your life was created from matter that became organized. Miniscule little fragments of matter coalesced with light/energy/spirit/intelligence to bring you your car, your spouse, your relationships, your job, all of your experiences, everything – the good and the not so good.

Some shamans say that when we're awake we're actually dreaming and when we sleep and dream at night, that's more of the literal reality of things. Confusing, no? **In essence, you're the dreamer dreaming this life of yours into reality – you, along with a bajillion other planetary tribe mates.** It can get confusing to figure out which part you're responsible for.

Everything we experience in our awakened reality here on planet Earth comes from the flowing river of energy, thoughts, words, and actions we take. That's what organizes matter and everything we create. Of course, there are many other beings doing the same thing. **You alone don't control the universe, but you can control the part you contribute to the whole.**

Yeah, I know. That all sounds pretty strange. You may be wondering what the heck I'm talking about. Nobody's told you about this strange river. Well, it's a secret, but now you're in on it. And, believe me, you want to know about this EPIC river, because I know you want to create beautiful and wondrous experiences and connections.

```
Fire up your inner stoke factory.
   You were born for awesomeness.
  (Every elephant knows this.)
```

" *Alice*

To work in the EPIC arena, where the hero is you, you must find the river within yourself. "How the heck do I do that?" Well, that river is always there. Everyone has a connection to that EPIC inner river – but it may be all covered by brush or it may be dried up or hidden from your awareness. Mine was. It's part of your EPIC journey to find that river inside.

The quickest path to finding your own connection to the EPIC river is best discovered by you. To get started, try listening to music you connect to; reading poetry or other writing you find inspiring; moving your body through dance, running, or yogurt (that's what I call yoga, because I still rebel against its seriousness just a tiny bit) – or take your quest more literally and go to an actual river. **See what happens as you sit on the riverbank or plunge into the water.** Any or all of those paths and many others (you choose!) can help in different ways to keep you in touch with that EPIC river. I use them all.

Revel in the DELICIOUS DELIGHTS
you stumble onto daily. Most people
are just having an ordinary day.

Dig what's extraordinary.

" *Alice*

When you can sense that EPIC river within, you'll find a place of utter peace, inner quietness, and solitude. Then, while you're there, **think about where you want your life to go, who you'd like to take along on this fun ride, and how you're going to do it.** This is big. As singer Jason Mraz said, "They're waiting for YOU to say, 'This is what I'm going to do and this is how I'm going to do it and this is who I'm bringing along,' and the minute you say that, everyone's like 'YAY, let's go!'"

You really can't get things wrong when you create from that EPIC place, which you do before anything has actually happened. Don't spend time focusing on stuff you've already created (unless it's good stuff). Go to your inner river and focus on what is yet to be. What would be fantastic? How would it feel? Exploring in that way is how the matter of the universe creates along with you.

As the EPIC things you dreamed of start showing up in your life, celebrate. Then keep going. Dream further.

❀❀ What would be EPIC to create next?

❀❀ What do you need to do to make space and time for going to that inner EPIC river of yours?

 IS FOR

FAIL

Some days are like surfing perfect wave after perfect wave. We enjoy every single minute. Such days can be so absolutely, bafflingly delightful that we begin to wonder what the heck is going on. Other days simply suck. They feel like a FAIL. It can be hard to be a FREAK, as we're so tuned in to the frequencies of our days. The highs are exceedingly high and the lows can feel devastatingly low. We wonder what's causing the ruckus. Is it the planetary energy? **Did I miscalculate my numerology? Was it that spiritual donut I ate?**

SPIRITUAL DONUT *Sprouted-grain toast slathered with coconut oil and orange blossom honey.*

I've learned that as fucking amazing and incredible as some days are, there are also days that feel like a FAIL. At such times, I advise becoming aware as soon as possible of the darkness descending and immediately activating any kind of FEEL GOOD you can – **listen to music you love, go out in nature, snuggle a pug, or put yourself to bed.** Some days, I do all of that and I still feel the FAIL, at least until I fall into un-consciousness on my Tempur-Pedic mattress.

Perfectionism comes with the territory.
It can be frustrating when something
falls short of your vision.

Let it go or let somebody else do
the fussing so you can get back
to creating something new.

" *Alice*

There's a concept I've come to understand about this FAIL process that helps me relax more about it: When we feel that looming sense of doom, FAIL, or uh-oh, when things that were going great all of a sudden go south, **it's simply our own personal cosmic-energy rubber band pulling back.** If we can hang in there as peacefully as possible, without thrashing, we can anticipate FEEL GOODs ahead as the rubber band's cycle turns. Everything changes. If we hang on, we may soon be sent slingshot-style straight into cosmic delight again.

THRASHING *can consist of anything that fights against the FAIL feeling, like getting angry, resisting, taking uninspired action, or perseverating about bad things.*

PERSEVERATE *To insistently prolong or repetitively think about something after it's passed or stopped. That "thing" is often something we have absolutely no way of controlling without harming ourselves (or others) in the process.*

Another beautiful metaphor for these harsh FAIL patches is surfing. Pipeline is a famous and dangerous surf spot in Hawaii known for its perfectly formed, powerful tubular waves. Apparently, right before you drop down into a Pipeline wave – a beautiful tube of divine swirling, cycling sea water forming a time-suspended and encircling space – there's a woolly patch. **Immediately before dropping into the smooth, glorious portion of the Pipeline wave, it can get hairy.** It's like the cosmic rubber band being pulled back before the slingshot into FEEL GOOD.

To increase the certainty of navigating the woolly bit and entering that glorious space, be Zen inside your brain. Surfers who Hang 10 – walk to the front of the board while surfing and hang all ten toes over the edge – need a Zen-like focus, a quiet and peaceful mind. If you can't get into that Hang 10 Zen space, you can't hang on. You'll fall out of the wave and risk a bad wipeout. But if you can Hang 10 with Zen, your energy will merge with the wave's energy. You'll become one with what is. It won't be you riding the wave, but you and the wave creating a mutual experience together.

> Sink into your bewilderment
> for 3-5 minutes. Then go right
> back to being kick-ass.
>
> " *Alice*

Get through your own woolly patches the same way. The next time you feel FAIL coming on, remember that you have choices. Start with simply finding a way to feel a tad better. Become quiet in your mind, dance, cry, listen to music that feels good, find a friend, meditate, run fast, walk slow, or, if all else fails, sleep it off. Remember that it's just your cosmic rubber band exercising itself. You're about to enter a better place ... if you can just Hang 10 with Zen a bit longer.

sarah bamford seidelmann m.d. | www.borntoFREAK.com

❀❀ When have you smelled FAIL and transmuted it into a wonderful experience by Hanging 10 with Zen?

❀❀ What did you do that transmuted the experience?

Permit yourself occasional
lionish bouts of moodiness,
but never lose track of your
precious inner jackass.

" Alice

Allow Myself to Introduce Myself

CLIFF
JUMPER

CLIFF JUMPER

On more than one occasion, people have told me how brave I am, saying they wouldn't be able to do some of the things I've done, like travel to rural Africa, quit my job, adopt a baby, completely switch careers at midlife, tell people that I work with animal totems and talk with the spirits in my shamanic work. My reply is always the same: I couldn't not do those things. Not to be dramatic, but not doing them would have killed me.

I'm a cliff jumper at heart. I'm an action-taker, one who enjoys leaping for leaping's sake, to see what might happen. I love taking risks. Not dangerous risks, mind you, at least not to me. They're well-thought-out risks. **The risks that thrill me always involve going after a heart's desire while not being a hundred percent sure it will work out.** Maybe being only fifty percent sure (math is not my strong suit).

Sometimes, the thing we want most is something we can't seem to have. At one point, that was the case for me. All I'd ever wanted to be was a mom. I'd been in training forever. By age four, I was begging to be allowed to hold any baby I was near. I had dozens of dolls that were dressed and accessorized in real human baby clothes. Every Sunday, I helped Mrs. Grickas, our Episcopalian church's babysitter, with diapering, rocking, chasing, and entertaining. I studied baby care in books at the library. I babysat my way through junior high and high school. **Kids just lit me up. I was loopy banana pancakes for them.**

When Mark and I got serious about starting a family, I figured it would be a snap. **"Bamfords get pregnant as easily as falling off logs,"** my Mother had ominously said throughout my teen and college years. For Mark and me, that wasn't the case. We thought perhaps it was due to the stress of going through our medical residencies.

After much trying on our own and many treatments and evaluations, we found out that I had Stage 4 endometriosis and Mark had some kind of sperm antibodies. We then tried all manner of things to deal with those circumstances, including a round of in vitro fertilization (IVF) and a home equity loan. None of it worked. Though I got pregnant a few times, every time it ended with an early miscarriage. The doctors encouraged us to keep going, to keep trying. We were *so young*, they told us. It should work.

In my sadness and confusion I finally went to a support group for infertile myrtles. That night, as I watched and listened to people recounting their EPIC tales of woe (ten IVFs, no money, lost homes, spouses who wouldn't agree to various methods), I realized something simple and profound: I want to be a mother! Good Gawwwd, I didn't want to end up like one of those people in the group – hopeless, out of money, and absolutely miserable, with no apparent way out. But I didn't need to get pregnant to be a mother!

I ran out of that support group with my sparkling clarity and went right home and told Mark I wanted to start adoption proceedings immediately. He, of course, was not ready. (I was born ready.) Eventually, he got ready, and adopting is what we did.

Becoming a parent is like going on a blind date that lasts forever. Having a kid biologically is like jumping off a cliff (though few of us seem to realize that). Adopting is like jumping off a cliff that's a bit higher. Adopting kids was one of the biggest cliffs we've ever jumped off, and, wow, are we glad we did it.

I leapt from other cliffs after that one. The month before my six-month sabbatical from pathology practice was up (and with my husband's full support), I decided not to return to work as a physician. At that point, I was already in the midst of writing my first book, I was coaching alongside master coaches, and I'd launched my first surfing retreat in Hawaii with some of my fellow coaches. **It had all happened so quickly, the way things do when we're on the right path.** I'd gotten a lot of green lights telling me to *Go!*

> Screw mastery. Just get out there and
> give it a go. It's how you learn.
>
> " *Alice*

And yet I was still scared to make the big leap of not returning to work as a physician. I knew I could no longer turn my back on my life's calling to heal souls and be a coach, but making lots of money had always equaled power and success to me. That wasn't too strange, given our culture and my upbringing.

As I searched for the answer, I realized that while money was nice, it didn't solve the problems of the heart, and my heart longed for healing and connection. I wanted to help others heal and I wanted to try fully expressing myself in the world, whatever the haystacks that was going to look like. Could I do that and make enough money to help support our family? Perhaps more importantly, could my ego surrender and let my husband support me while I pursued my own dreams?

The answer was *yes*. I jumped. And it's been incredible. It's difficult to put into words how beautiful my life is now and how much I love the work I get to do. My life is not always easy or simple, but it's deeply satisfying down to the level of my soul. Yes, there are still dragons to slay. New fears keep coming up as I approach new cliffs, but when I sit in silence and ask for guidance, the answers that come are always crystal clear. So I **keep striding deeper and deeper into my life, leaping off new cliffs, knowing less and trusting more.** And that feels very good.

sarah bamford seidelmann m.d. | www.borntoFREAK.com

IS FOR GOADING

Math is mostly boring to me, unless it's lifemath, like this:

Regular Life = Risks

For me, the most important lifemath equation is this:

Amazing Life = Risks + GOADING

What's so great about GOADING? A **GOAD** is something that urges. Significantly, one of the definitions of **GOADING** has to do with using a sharp, pointy stick to herd domestic animals with a painful poke. "Hey!?" you say, "That sounds like it would hurt. I thought you were a life coach, not a sadomasochist!"

Some life coaches use GOADING, others offer you a couch. You gotta pick your poison. I – as I suspect many do who were born to FREAK – prefer to be GOADED. To get the things done that matter the most to me, I need to GOAD myself on a regular basis or I need to find someone who's willing to GOAD me.

Go at your own pace.
But get the hell up and get going.

"

One way of self-GOADING is to create immediacy and a sense of the EPIC (see "E is for EPIC"), like by stating out loud, in public, what you intend to do. For example, I once said out loud, "I'm going to the Kumba Mela in India in 2013 to live in an eco-hut on the Ganges River for 21 days at the largest gathering of humanity in the world." After I said it, I realized strangers were staring at me with sincere concern and reaching slowly, stealthily, like Navy SEALs, for their cell phones to call security. Then I thought, **Oh, dagnabbit all to hell! Did I really just say that out loud in the produce section of the new co-op?** Yep, I sure did. And I do want to go to the Mela with sixty million other kooks, despite the fact that it scares the bejesus out of me and is illogical and entirely banana pancakes.

I committed to the Kumba Mela when I felt true divine inspiration to do so. In a red-hot moment, following careful consideration, I paid my nonrefundable deposit. Sometimes, committing is very good for FREAKS. It keeps us from having a back door to sneak out of to avoid doing something big that we truly (heart and soul) want to experience. That's not to say that we can't bail if an experience begins to feels unsafe or if circumstances change significantly. We always have choices.

It's later than you think.
Seize inspiration.
GOAD yourself and be GOADED.

" Alice

Another form of GOADING is wanting to create something that excites you so much that life itself gets exciting and wonderful. Since 1967, I've been GOADING myself and others in this way, with ever-decreasing mercy.

What happens without GOADING? **"Why, Sarah,"** you ask, **"must I be prodded with sharp, pointy thingies?"** Well, they don't have to be super pointy. I've discovered, though, that if I let inspiration and enthusiasm pass by without harnessing it, without using it to somehow GOAD myself into commitment and action, often nothing will actually ever happen. That's not horrifying, and yet nothing ever happening doesn't usually lead to an Amazing Life (see lifemath above).

Experts say the statistical chance of being born into a human body is about as slim as stepping in rocking horse feces. If that's true, then this is your moment! You're here. Do something! Do whatever it takes to follow through with what you want to do.

My hunch is that without access to quality GOADING, many of us who were born to FREAK get stuck. The inspiration arrives for writing the song, taking the class, creating the painting or the blog, inventing a kale-rific pasta recipe, launching a business ... but we let it pass by because we've lost faith that we'll actually follow through and finish. **We remember scores of unfinished projects and unfulfilled commitments left in our FREAKY wakes.**

Maybe we've been told by some self-appointed authority that we have no right to do what we're excited to do. Or we've become so disconnected from our true selves – from years of self-abuse or obsessing over what everybody else needs – that we don't even know what we want anymore. **If that's the case** for you, do not walk but run (calmly and without scissors), to an Al-Anon meeting, which could be a useful form of GOADING for you.

AUTHORITY FIGURES *Anyone who tells you that you can't do what you want to do deep down in your soul, is just plain fucking wrong, incorrect, or otherwise in error. Avoid such "authority" figures like the plague ... until you actually do the thing they told you that you couldn't do. Then show up, forgive them, and give them a hug. Realize that they probably weren't having a good day the day they said "Nope, you can't do it."*

The key about using GOADING is to first notice how a potential risk feels, deep down in your core. If it feels like a *maybe* or a *sort of*, if you feel wishy-washy about it, **like a wet, limp washcloth flopping over the tub spigot,** then this is not the thing to go all GOADY with yourself over.

On the other hand, if the feeling you have, deep down, about a potential risk is a true "Hell, yes!" or, even better, a "YEEEUUSSSS!!," then it's a big thing, a worthy thing, and it's likely to require self-GOADING (making the deposit, buying the ticket) ... plus additional talent. Call in your cavalry to assist. **Muster the babysitters, dog sitters, DJs, bike rental agencies, systems experts, helicopter pilots, bouncers, and professional GOADERS** (the life-coach type, not the life-couch type). Often, when you feel that deep-down YES!, such people will appear magically.

Get help polishing big important projects.
So your ideas get seen in the best light.

"*Alice*

sarah bamford seidelmann m.d. | www.borntoFREAK.com

I have a Bo Peep–like editor, Grace, who gently GOADS me like I'm a sheep (she also uses herding techniques as an extra bonus), with her giant (but humanely used) shepherd's crook. I like being a sheep in her crook. Her GOADING consists of gentle reminder emails or notes on my drafts in Google Docs that are very polite. GOADING can be surprisingly gentle yet still very effective as it urges us onward.

G**RACE'S GOADING** *Here is an example of Grace's polite GOADING: "If you want to actually get this done, you may want to limit the number of chapters to 73. Also, please don't move files without first checking with me. I have a system. Love, Grace."*

I delight in GOADING other humans to do things that serve their fabulous souls. I think this is why people on buses tend to sidle up to me and share strange things that I suspect they wouldn't share with just anyone. **People often seem to intuitively know that I was born FREAKY,** and so they feel comfortable freely sharing their own wondrous FREAKINESS with me.

They confess that they've been brooding about buying an RV and cruising the continent studying dog costume designers, but they're allergic to dogs. Or they let it spill that **they've always wanted to climb K2 and have been doing deep lunges around their backyard at dawn, but worry that it's probably too late.** Or they confess in a whisper that deep inside them lives a take-no-prisoners chef they've kept under wraps and they're considering applying to Le Cordon Bleu next year when their kid enters high school.

Many of our eccentric yearnings make no earthly sense, even to the person who harbors them. I believe it's especially important to pay attention when a desire is so strange that it mystifies you or you have no idea why you feel compelled to do it (please keep it legal). If you have a persistent eccentric yearning, it's likely to be coming from a very high place, somewhere above the clouds, from the layers of otherworldliness, and this is very good. Accept it. You're being compelled to take a risk toward something important. ... and, **most likely, you must be GOADED (Amazing Life = Risks + GOADING).**

When people share their eccentric, compelling, risky ideas, I go wild with excitement. I can see what they want, and now I want them to have it, too. I can sense how the world will be that much richer if they do it. Then I GOAD. **I GOAD because the more people express their own brand of awesomeness and beauty, the better things get.** We gain new services, creations, experiences, and fantasticness to feel good about.

Though I live to GOAD, I try very hard to GOAD only if I've gotten permission to GOAD, because **without permission GOADING doesn't work. It just bounces off or mildly irritates, like Retin-A.** Some people report that they actually dig being GOADED by me. (Mary, don't make me come over there and open up a can of GOADING whoop-ass. If you're reading this, put this book down right now and go work on your children's book.)

> Ganesha, the elephant-headed Hindu god, isn't called "Remover of Obstacles" for nothing, you know. Elephants know how to get stuff done. Our process can be a tad messy but, believe me, we get where we want to go.
>
> " *Alice*

So, find a way to get GOADED. GOAD yourself or have someone else do it. Or both. Announce your plans. Search for the cavalry you'll need. GOAD other FREAKS and kooks like yourself. Get out there and make the world a better place.

What's calling to you from above the clouds, way up in the stratosphere?

What do you need GOADING help about?

Who could open that can of GOADING whoop-ass for you?

IS FOR

HOCUS - POCUS FOCUS

The word *focus* can be scary for those of us who were born to FREAK, especially if we've been told we should focus on one thing to the exclusion of all the other stuff we delight in. As in, "You need to grow up and chose a profession. Decide what you want to be already! Veterinarian? Artist? Lawyer? Firefighter? Stay-at-home mom?" **But (you wonder) can't I be all of those?**

Focus **can also be a horrific trigger word, bringing up bad memories of people shouting "You need to focus!!"** (like when we were supposed to be focusing on trigonometry but instead were staring outside at something beautiful). Not to be overly dramatic, but **focusing can feel like metaphoric death for FREAKS,** simply because we may feel more *alive* when we're free to focus on many things simultaneously – taking it all in, becoming one with it all.

I call our born-to-FREAK, magical, taking-it-all-in ability to focus *HOCUS-POCUS FOCUS*. It's a hyper-attentive way we merge and become one with something – a project, a topic, a situation, anything.

This natural ability has a dark side. We see it when we're so merged with something that the waffles burn and we don't hear the children shouting until their voices get really loud and urgent ("Mom. Mom. MOM. MOM! *MOMMMMM!!!*").

HOCUS-POCUS FOCUS is a gift to be wielded with care. It can have a rawwwther tenacious quality to it. We can hyper-lock onto a single thing. Like the honey badger's, our HOCUS-POCUS FOCUS can be fierce and difficult to unlock. If our magical focus is misdirected or if we fail to unlock at critical points, we can get burned and cause mayhem.

THE HONEY BADGER *The honey badger is one of the most ferocious animals on the planet. They plunge into bee-infested underground caves in search of honey. They bite off the heads of poisonous vipers. Sometimes they get bitten by vipers and injected with venom and have to sleep it off. It's all in a day's work for the average honey badger. No big whoop. La di dah.*

As you may have noticed, I like to look on the bright side. When HOCUS-POCUS FOCUS is grounded in reality, it can make for some pretty miraculous performances — in the operating room, the chemistry lab, the art studio, or the kitchen. When properly applied and grounded, HOCUS-POCUS FOCUS is like channeling the universe.

> Let approximately 92% of your brilliant ideas drift off like dandelion seeds into the wind.
>
> " *Alice*

How can we best ground HOCUS-POCUS FOCUS to bring on magic and miracles without unwanted mayhem? The trick is to take in all the information we're receiving – being really open to inspiration and messages from the universe – and then find ways to take action on the bits we find most inspiring.

Nurture the other 8% of your ideas,
the ideas that seem RIDICULOUS and
ILLOGICAL, but feel like love -
so exciting and deeply satisfying
that you can't NOT do them.

" Alice

For example, when using my HOCUS-POCUS FOCUS to create a fabulous, inspiring meal, I might begin by looking around to **assess the ingredients I have on hand**. Then I bring on the magic. My mind starts running through **all sorts of ideas and combinations**. What meal could I make with broccoli, shallots, smoked salmon, and fresh ginger? Questions come up. Do we have basmati rice? Cilantro? How much time do I have? At some point, I ask my body a question: **What would taste really good right now?** Finally, **I begin to narrow my options and prepare for action.** Which idea has the most verve? Do I need help? Are there shortcuts? ... And eventually, **dinner is served**. The results are often fantastic and always interesting. I almost never cook the same thing in exactly the same way. By the time we eat, the kitchen usually looks like a bomb has gone off in it, but fellow diners with happy tummies tend to be glad to help with the cleanup.

As a practicing pathologist I used HOCUS-POCUS FOCUS all the time to plow through stacks of slides at my microscope, tuning out all distractions so I could tune in to what I was seeing, noticing, and sensing about a patient's slide. I learned that my HOCUS-POCUS FOCUS was strongest and best from 7:30 a.m. to about noon. In that place of utter focus, I didn't enjoy interruptions because they messed with my delicious zone of complete focus hyper-lock. I feel the same way when I'm writing.

> Be cool with your own BEST WORKING
> conditions. Own how you roll best
> and honor it daily.
>
> " *Alice*

HOCUS-POCUS FOCUS keeps many of us happily engaged in our life's work, allowing us to tune out the noise of the world and tune in to our own genius. When in service to a true heart's desire, HOCUS-POCUS FOCUS can get the book published, the art masterpiece completed, the unusual diagnosis slam-dunked, the marathon finish line crossed, the patient stabilized, or the very first Tiki and Tennis Pasta Party planned and executed in style.

Do take care when using HOCUS-POCUS FOCUS, as wielding it is like waving a laser around, and you don't want to get burned. Learn to point the laser at what matters most. Using HOCUS-POCUS FOCUS on things that captivate but don't serve – like watching or listening to media that make you feel dispirited, doing projects that go against your personal truths, or doing work that's not deeply satisfying – can take you to some very unhappy places. HOCUS-POCUS FOCUS is fierce. Notice when it's time to turn it off.

It's doubtful that we can avoid HOCUS-POCUS FOCUS perils entirely, but **simply being aware of the need to be aware goes a long way toward helping**.

When you know you'll need to come out of your HOCUS-POCUS FOCUS to pay attention to something else, like taking care of daily life so it supports you, you may need to hire spotters or bodyguards or get a kitchen timer. Perhaps a beeping alarm can remind you that it's time to take the haggis out of the oven so you don't burn down the house, or alert you when it's time to get ready for your next client appointment.

**Use your FREAKY superpowers
(like HOCUS-POCUS FOCUS)
for the good.**

" *Alice*

Embrace who you are and figure out what works for you to help you stay grounded so you have a strong base for your natural HOCUS-POCUS FOCUS skills. **And know when to dismount.**

 Are you aware of it when you go into HOCUS-POCUS FOCUS mode?

 What are some of the ways your ability to HOCUS-POCUS FOCUS has served you?

 What are some ways you can stay grounded or get help when you need to focus on something you're not thrilled about having to focus on?

A Cautionary Tale

Being HOCUS-POCUS FOCUSED on things you love can create some interesting situations. Allow me to illustrate with a cautionary tale.

On safari in Africa, as I was on my way out the door to hop in the Land Rover and go check out some Beasties, I quickly grabbed what I thought was the right pill and slammed it down with water. As I swallowed, it was like I was doing it in s-l-o-w m-o-t-i-o-n, because I suddenly realized I'd just accidentally swallowed an Ambien instead. I was so HOCUS-POCUS FOCUSED (can you say *tunnel vision*?) on what I LOVED (going on safari, YAY!) that I missed the label details on the pill bottles.

AMBIEN *was developed as a fast-acting sedative, designed to put you to sleep quickly, keep you asleep, and give you a deep rest. Many people take it on extended international flights, as it helps prevent jet lag, but without ill effects. For that purpose, it's fantastic. I used one on the way to Africa and had only minimal jet lag.*

I hate to throw up, especially on purpose, so I had to stick it out. I don't remember most of that day, but I apparently had a very interesting time. I was told later that everyone else in the Land Rover found me fascinating. I do remember staring at a leopard for what seemed like an interminably long time.

sarah bamford seidelmann m.d. | www.borntoFREAK.com

Though not documented in the pharmacology literature, **Ambien causes you to behave like Eloise at the Plaza**. In no uncertain terms, I announced my feelings about that rawwwther boring leopard to my companions (a fabulously super-model-gorgeous German family) in the open-topped Land Rover and then I stood up, which is a big no-no in the bush, as the wild Beasties may consider a break in the Land Rover's normal silhouette to be a threat. They're often only ten feet away (or even less), so if they feel threatened they could pretty easily leap up and devour you. With a kind but forceful yank, my friend Suzi quickly pulled me back into my seat before the leopard noticed me.

ELOISE AT THE PLAZA *Eloise is an irrepressible little girl who's the main character in the* Eloise *book series. This little girl was truly born to FREAK, so if you want delightful books to read to yourself or to some kids about what fun a FREAK can have with the full support of the staff of a luxury hotel, check her out.*

Being soft-bodied humans rather than invincible gods, we actually do occasionally need to focus on stuff that doesn't interest us, at least long enough to be safe and function in society. We need to take the right pill while on safari, pay the bills, brush and floss, and listen and respond to hollering children who need us.

the end

I IS FOR IRREPRESSIBLE

Life can be dry and dull, but good Gawwwd, why let it be? IRREPRESSIBILITY seems to be a common feature of those of us who were born to FREAK.

This is what living the quality of IRREPRESSIBILITY is like: **No matter how hard you try, you can't suppress a hundred percent of the wild, wondrous churnings inside of you**. Being IRREPRESSIBLE may result in blurting things out spontaneously, swearing loudly, doing headstands (when headstands are very obviously not called for), laughing at strange moments, shouting and dancing with abandon when it's obvious to non-FREAKS that it would be best to whisper and stand still. Et cetera.

SUPPRESSION *Trying hard to suppress your IRREPRESSIBLE nature may result in chronic disease, pain, suffering, addiction, and other forms of great distress. Trust me on this one. Or experiment on yourself and find out.*

**Don't dabble in dangerous addictions.
Help is out there, dear humans. Reach for it.**

" *Alice*

Most medical school professors I met while going through training as a physician were introverted types who enjoyed the symphony, a good Sudoku, and quiet nights at home, but **my favorite professor in the hallowed halls of medical school was an Irishman with a very large head** (circumferentially), who said outrageous, silly, and shocking things. He was, in a word, IRREPRESSIBLE.

Sometimes I wonder whether he was the only reason I was drawn to study tiny things through microscopes. In those pre-Photoshop days, he spent hundreds of hours searching for and photographing patterns in clustered white blood cells loaded with bacteria, which he'd then use to create letters and spell words. Later, during an after-class party, he'd ask unsuspecting students over to look at his microscopic photographs. "How do you think this patient contracted the infection?" he'd ask. Baffled, the students would peer with great intellectual interest at the images of clumped patterns of bacteria. The professor would cackle and snort to himself with laughter (IRREPRESSIBLY). Using patterns of clumped-up bacteria known to be sexually transmitted, he had cleverly spelled out "FUCKING." Once you realized the joke was on you, you laughed and howled along with him. In his presence, learning about potentially dry topics became absolutely scintillating (and a bit naughty).

**Smile maniacally at others during
working hours. It's disarming.**

" *Alice*

Of course, he offended nearly as many people as he entertained. To those of us who loved him, **he was a beacon of bright and hysterical light in a dark cave of lectures that seemed endlessly bleak**.

Successful comedians leverage their IRREPRESSIBILITY, saying onstage the outrageous stuff many of us keep trapped inside our heads. As Tracy Morgan of *Saturday Night Live* and *30 Rock* fame says, **"If you're not offending somebody, you're just not funny, period."**

If you were born to FREAK (and clearly you were), then you've probably experienced a lifetime of being shushed and told to simmer down. Someone has likely pleaded with you to "Please just be normal." **Perhaps you've felt urges come from deep within that you sensed you should repress, as they might not be socially acceptable**. You have to decide for yourself what feels good to express.

I've learned that my own IRREPRESSIBILITY is what most people *love* about me. It's also what I love about other people. **I like to wear strange hats with octopi on them, talk to strangers, shout "WAHOOO!" as I jump into a cold lake**, ask a LOT of questions, raise my hand and volunteer, try new things, say out loud what I'm thinking, and address the elephant(s) in the room.

The more IRREPRESSIBLE I am with my work, the better my work is. Even in a field as wild and untamed as life coaching, I've noticed a tendency for people to be quite serious, as in "There's a correct and proper way to do this." Hmmm. Maybe not. Some of the most powerful coaching I've witnessed has come about through pure love and big doses of humor and IRREPRESSIBILITY.

sarah bamford seidelmann m.d. | www.borntoFREAK.com

Own your point of view.
If you're not offending someone,
you may not be stating it strongly enough.

" *Alice*

I've learned not to hold back, or to hold back less. **IRREPRESSIBILITY, when expressed, has the potential to make people laugh. It can melt hearts.** It entertains. It gives others more permission to be free and unrepressed. Sure, there's a chance we may offend (though that's never my aim). To truly be your fully FREAKED self, you have to be willing to take that chance.

✿✿ What if your IRREPRESSIBILITY was a gift?

✿✿ How could you be more IRREPRESSIBLE?

✿✿ How can you celebrate your own and others' IRREPRESSIBLE nature?

When singing is not what
the situation calls for, sing LOUDLY.
Ditto with dancing, snorting, standing
on your head, and hugging.

" *Alice*

Allow Myself to Introduce Myself

TIGGER

TIGGER

As a child, I had an enormous amount of energy and enthusiasm. I still do. At age five, when I was first exposed to A. A. Milne's *Winnie the Pooh*, I immediately recognized myself in Tigger. **Tiggers like to bounce.**

I also recognized that not everyone enjoyed Tigger's impressive enthusiasm and buoyant nature. My mother, whose energy level was approximately 872 percent lower than mine (on average), relied on a couple of different things to save her sanity (and some of my hide) where I and my great bounciness were concerned.

> If you're feeling unbalanced,
> let off some steam. Move your carcass!
>
> " *Alice*

One sanity-saver was the pool in our backyard in Hollywood, Florida, where we lived for a few years. I swam in that pool for hours every day. When we moved to Minnesota and left the pool behind, I spent lots of time bouncing around in the massive system of creeks I discovered near our home.

My mother, who's more like Rabbit in *Winnie the Pooh* – slightly exasperated and anxious around all that bouncing – brilliantly enrolled me in classes or activities I was interested in. I took dance classes, swimming classes, and whatever else I wanted to.

Every Saturday, from eight in the morning to four in the afternoon, I lived at the YMCA. I loved the Y and was so stoked to be there. We did arts and crafts, like copper enameling and making clay pots that we fired in giant kilns. We swam. We ran around like banshees, under the supervision of some fine young adults. At noon, we got to eat pizza, drink *swamp water* (three kinds of soda mixed together), and watch a film. The quality of the films varied tremendously, but the pizza and swamp water had ineffable, wonderful qualities I could always count on.

As a kid, I swam, packed and ate picnics, put on shows, played doctor, dressed up, made forts, rearranged the furniture, cooked things, collected stuff, and listened to music. Strangely enough (or perhaps not so strangely), those are the very same activities I have fun doing now – though the locations, ingredients, objects, and musicians have changed.

My Tigger-ish super high activity level and great irrepressibility have resulted in quite a few injuries over the years: broken arms, fingers, and collar bones, sprained wrists and ankles. Ace bandages and various braces lay around my childhood bedroom in heaps, ready to protect the latest blows and defend against new ones. Getting banged up is sometimes par for the course for those of us who were born to FREAK.

In high school, my great inner bounciness and love of adventure led me to try just about every activity possible at least once: swim team, flag-twirling, Knowledge Bowl, student council, drama club, swing choir. I was the team mascot (a bear). I was a hockey cheerleader **(yes, doing the splits on ice is just as tough as you'd think it would be)**. I was even an informal aerobics instructor. I fancied myself a bit of a Jane Fonda, **practicing my skills in the furnace room at night – the only place in the house it was warm enough to don Lycra in the northern Minnesota wintertime.** I erratically held aerobics classes in the choir room at school, for others with high energy levels.

By bouncing through all those activities, I learned about all sorts of humans: artists, jocks, intellectuals, and flag-twirlers.

These days, my inner Tigger is kept happy through daily romps in the woods, dancing to pop music, trying out new things (like surfing), and taking my kids on various daily adventures.

```
You have a love for the R-U-S-H. Just don't
let that chaos-craving part of you (the part
that feels most at peace in the eye of the
tempest) hurt a relationship or destroy a
beautiful equilibrium that exists.
```

" *Alice*

Like many of us who were born to FREAK, I have enormous amounts of energy and enthusiasm, especially when I'm feeling good. I feel good when I'm getting love and enough rest, when I'm being creative, and when I'm expressing myself.

Though I've been shushed and told I need to **pipe down, slow down, stop bouncing, and simmer down** many a time by the Eeyores in life, I try to remember that **bouncing is what I do best.**

J IS FOR

JONESING

Many of us FREAKS are intense people who feel things deeply, madly, and passionately, right down to our very core. This intensity of feeling is what makes FREAKS FREAKY and wonderful. Our intense feelings sometimes show up as a JONES: a craving, an urge, a deeply felt need that's very right-now-ish.

> Become stoked.
> Frost your lifecake.
>
> " *Alice*

When you feel a JONES coming on, it can be a need for one of two things. It's important to know which of the two it is.

A JONES can be:

1) a desire to escape the discomfort you're currently experiencing, or
2) a desire for something that's your true heart's desire.

     sarah bamford seidelmann m.d. | www.borntoFREAK.com

Sometimes, the intensity of a feeling pouring through the pores of a FREAK can initiate a bout of JONESING as a diversion.

This kind of JONESING is an intense longing to escape, a desire to avoid or subvert the strong feelings we're experiencing, such as pain, anger, sadness, fear, or distress. This is why many FREAKS fall into the arms of addiction, JONESING their way unhealthily through life via food, drugs, spending, sex, and more. I'm not talking about drinking a glass of wine (according to my mother, "A glass of wine can maketh the heart glad" ... unless ye are an alcoholic), eating an occasional dime-bag of chocolate chip cookies, or reading Fifty Shades of Grey and getting inspired to buy some rope. It's when you let JONESING run your life, exchanging unhealthy activities for life-affirming feel-good activities, that there's a problem.

ADDICTION *means doing something over and over again (shopping, sex, drugs, alcohol, TV, knitting), despite the fact that there's a negative consequence (isolation, self-loathing, poor health, job loss, house loss, marriage implosion, death, an excess of sweaters).*

A JONES can also be a deep desire for something that's a true heart's desire.

When you feel a JONESING coming on, stop for a moment and ask yourself which kind of JONESING it is. Is the urgent urge that's bubbling up, one that will move you toward the fulfillment of your heart's desires? Or is it a need to be distracted from the present moment, to escape from the discomfort of a feeling, or to avoid dealing with what's going on?

Creative Energy = Sexual Energy = Energy. Do not, under any circumstances, do the math. Just use that energy with people and projects you love.

 " *Alice*

Addiction needs to be distinguished from the odd self-soothing habits we FREAKS sometimes have, the habits and activities and mannerisms we engage in to soothe ourselves — like pacing, rocking, singing, listening to music, chewing gum, nibbling on fingers, twirling hair. FREAKS often work best under odd conditions — wrapped in blankets, hidden under the dining room table, in economy class on an oversold flight to Mumbai. Heck, Temple Grandin built a gentling contraption so she could apply the proper pressure to her body to help herself calm down, and look what amazing contributions she made to society!

T**EMPLE GRANDIN** *is an amazing, born-to-FREAK woman who's autistic. She used her unique sensitivities and visionary designs to revolutionize the way cattle facilities are built, creating better conditions for cattle and lowering costs of production.*

When it's not harmful, I say do whatever's needed to make yourself feel comfy and get things done. Get peaceful so you can FREAK. Whatever works, work it.

So, how do you know which kind of JONESING you're experiencing? Well, at first it may not be all that damn easy to figure out (I still sometimes get into weird JONESING episodes that perplex me), but **if you pause to ask why and keep asking,**

you're likely to get some useful answers. You're also more likely to get what you really want.

Here's an example – one of my oddest JONESING episodes:

I recently had a JONES for chickens, the kind that lays eggs in a henhouse. First, it was a little twinkle of a desire, but then it grew into more than a twinkle. It became intense. Finally, as Christopher Walken says in the infamous *Saturday Night Live* "More Cowbell" skit, "I got a fevah and the only prescription is more...."

> Be a student of absurdity.
> Tap into some whack-a-noodle. Doodle.
> There's magic in the impossible.
>
> " *Alice*

My JONES for chickens began when I saw an image of a henhouse in a magazine. **The next thing I knew I was at a holiday party drinking pear bellinis, and chicken talk was erupting into the conversation.** The lovely, chic host of the party (a FREAK, naturally), elegant in a ruffled silk blouse and narrow wool skirt, told me she'd been thinking about chickens. We were discussing how we're not really interested in book clubs. Instead of a book club, we said, **How about a chicken coop club? How much fun would that be?** We could drink champagne by our coops and discuss how things are going with our chickens. That sounded absolutely magical to me!

> Connection with like-minded
> humans does a FREAK good. Very good.
> Plan it or do it spontaneously, but do it!
>
> " *Alice*

BOOK CLUBS *First of all, it's too bossy. We don't really want to be told what books to read, especially if they're bad books we don't actually like. Secondly, having a book assigned feels too much like homework. Thirdly, when you go to a book club there are people who haven't actually read the book (I don't have any personal experience with book clubs, but I have this on good authority). According to multiple field reports, those nonreaders tend to be the people who talk the most about the book.*

Now, why on God's green Earth would I or anyone else want to have a champagne party at a chicken coop? It's just that 24 hours before our pear-bellini-infused chicken conversation, I'd stumbled onto a magazine photo that showed a lady in a ruffled white linen dress, a flower in her hair, and a stunningly beautiful chicken tucked under her arm. She stood in her chicken coop, which featured a crystal chandelier, a chair covered in distressed linen, and gorgeous feed sacks, which she'd probably imported from Europe. That image got stuck in my head. **Yes, I thought, there are going to be chickens.** I wasn't sure where I was going to get a white linen dress or how I was going to keep it clean, but the image of a chicken coop with a chandelier (or maybe a mirrored disco ball?) became firmly fixed in my head.

The madness had begun.

> Protect your ability to dream. It's a mad skill. Dream BIG. Then get ye olde tuckus off the couch and take action toward it. Daily.
>
> " *Alice*

I've learned that my JONESING must be handled with both presence of mind and curiosity. I also know by now that if I try to deny my JONESING, it only makes things worse. So I had to find a way to allow myself to safely explore *The Chicken Idea* until I knew whether it was an escape or my true heart's desire. To help myself decide, I bought a book about chickens, quizzed everyone I knew who had chickens, read blogs, and toured chicken coops. It was very, very fun. And, all the while, I asked myself why I was interested.

Fascinatingly, my chicken JONES appeared at a time when I'd just finished an EPIC project – writing my very first book, *What the Walrus Knows* – and was feeling a bit like a ship lost at sea ("Now what?"). It was actually *très* uncomfortable. The book launch party was over, I'd sold a bunch of books, but now we were into the Christmas season and I'd done all the talking and sharing and blogging I could do about the book without making my friends and family want to send me to Siberia for the holidays. So what was I to do next?

I'd hit the doldrums, and a FREAK can get very uncomfortable in the doldrums.

THE DOLDRUMS Doldrums *is a maritime term for the low-pressure area around the equator where a ship can get stuck for days or weeks because the wind has died down to nothing. This is not unlike post-stormy-excitement days, when a time of full-tilt metaphoric sailing stops, when the wind in our sails suddenly dies out, inspiration is lost, and we're not sure how the hell we're going to sail on. No ideas come. We're standing absolutely still.*

"Day after day, day after day,

We stuck, nor breath nor motion;

As idle as a painted ship

Upon a painted ocean."

– Samuel Taylor Coleridge

"The Rime of the Ancient Mariner"

Chickens seemed to be the answer to my doldrums. I could fill my discomforting days with activity, plans, ideas, things to learn, and chickens to pet! **I could avoid that awful stuck feeling and fill my sails with wind again (albeit chicken wind).** But as I felt my way into the chickens (pardon the visual), learning about the costs, the chores involved, and the additional duties added to the daily schedule ... I realized that it didn't feel good to go ahead with the chicken idea.

As I examined my chicken JONES, I saw that it was really a distraction from the work I was already committed to (caring for four kids, a dog, a parakeet, two Japanese fighter fish, and a coaching/healing practice). I allowed myself to keep feeling the uncomfortableness of not knowing what to do next, and I stayed open to what might come.

I came to believe that those chickens represented a desire to feel grounded, to make a new nest, to lay a few new eggs of my own, to dig into new creative projects and ideas. My real JONESING wasn't for chickens, but for something I found almost impossible to express in words. **Sort of a soft, hen-like desire for a new beloved creative project.**

After riding out the doldrums of January, I finally did find new wind for my sails, in the form of new projects to work on, but the chickens are still with me, reminding me of that journey. I love eggs and now I often buy ours from local hen owners, which deeply satisfies my chicken JONES.

Ask yourself what you're hoping your JONESING focus (topic, object, drink, food, person, experience, livestock) will bring you by following its call. If it will bring you inner peace, love, connection with other humans, or something else that feels deeply good, then GO FOR IT! If not, hang on for a bit with curiosity about what you're really craving beneath the JONES.

If you feel like JONESING has taken over your life and become unmanageable, I invite you to seek help from someone you trust. Take the first step toward filling your sails with fresh, healing breezes that will take you to your true heart's desires.

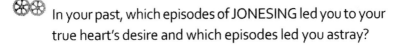 In your past, which episodes of JONESING led you to your true heart's desire and which episodes led you astray?

Are there any signs or signals that recur for you during JONESING episodes that help you know whether you're on the path of an addiction or a heart's desire?

Seek out activities that bring an inner smile (without the emotional hangover).

" *Alice*

Allow Myself to Introduce Myself

HUNTRESS

HUNTRESS

On the first day of medical school, with a gaze like a mountain lioness, I looked around the room at our class of fifty students and saw two men who were potential mates. I went home that night and reported my findings to my parents. One of the potential mates I'd homed in on turned out to be unavailable. The other, Mark, eventually become my husband. He really had no choice but to comply. I hunted him. I've heard tell of other women and men who felt as determined as I was about seeking out and pursuing their eventual mates.

Knowing what you want and going after it is extremely powerful.

My stalking courtship with Mark was rawwwther odd. I'd heard that Mark was on the soccer team, so I joined it, even though I'd never played soccer. The first night I showed up to play, I learned that Mark was out for the season because of an injury he'd sustained that evening. I quit the team on the spot and went and found Mark at the gym where he'd been injured. I helped him limp to his car. Later, we went on a series of dates.

> Get in touch with your ferocious
> leopardness, as required.

" Alice

I sensed that Mark and I were amazingly compatible – sparks were flying – and yet we didn't kiss or so much as cuddle on our first few dates. Have I mentioned that Mark was Lutheran and cautious by nature? By the sixth date, I was almost ready to throw in the towel.

As Mark tells it, I finally stopped talking long enough for him to lunge in for a kiss.

That evening, post-lunge, **we knocked a bunch of things off the walls and toppled some furniture**, including a record player, and our relationship was off to the races. Less than a year later, we got engaged.

Celebrate the fact that you may lunge
awkwardly (sexually and otherwise)
into conversations, ideas, and situations.
It's all part of the beauty of you.

As we rode the great whale of our medical education, plunging further and further out to sea with us attached, we clung to each other like barnacles.

My hunting has involved more than just landing my prospective husband. My mother can tell you that even when I was a kid, if I had my heart set on something, I was like a dog with a treasured bone. I simply would not give up.

Once I alighted on what interested me, I'd follow its trail in a steady, deliberate, relentless manner, learning and examining everything about it as I homed in. As I got closer and learned more, I'd either become more feverish, or I'd become less interested and abandon it altogether.

The things, people, ideas, and experiences that thrilled me most kept me on the prowl. I read, interviewed, assessed, reviewed, viewed, and examined every possible angle that intrigued me about whatever or whoever I was stalking. Even so, I didn't eventually capture everything I stalked. Many memorable and very exciting things got away from me: getting a horse of my own, having my own phone line, attending a boarding school for the arts during high school, or persuading my mother to have another baby at the age of forty. **Even mountain lions don't achieve a clean kill a hundred percent of the time.**

Some of the hunting I've done has led to fascinating experiences and beautiful projects, like **learning about the world of interior design**, interning with an interior designer, and completing several satisfying design projects; **exploring the world of philanthropy**, discovering what inspires others to give to worthy projects, and helping a few worthy projects get off the ground; and **delving into adoption and all its complexities** and deciding to create a family.

There's an old rule that we women should wait for Prince Charming to come to us, or that we shouldn't be the ones to pursue a mate. In my youth, I wondered whether it was okay for me to be the huntress. Now, when I hear wonderful stalker stories of other born-to-FREAK people going after and getting exactly what they want, it reminds me of how wonderful this multitude of mine is.

I continue to stalk prey of all kinds. This thrills me every day.

IS FOR

KERFUFFLE

KERFUFFLE *a disorderly outburst or raucous clattering, often involving children behaving like wild beasts*

In my dream life, I travel the world with my fantastic, stimulated, polite, engaging children and my dashing, enlightened husband. We eat exotic foods, gaze at great art, stroll foreign streets, and joyously make wonderful memories. The thing is, in my dream I tend to forget that there will almost always be a KERFUFFLE or two.

Knowing full well that a great life is full of KERFUFFLES can help those of us who were born to FREAK. It can help us not overreact or not become too disenchanted when life stops coming up roses for a while. I've learned to at least see a KERFUFFLE coming, if not to embrace it perfectly every time. **Here's the trick: Embrace the KERFUFFLE, then distance yourself.**

Allow me to illustrate ...

sarah bamford seidelmann m.d. | www.borntoFREAK.com

I decided to pursue my vision of a dream life by taking a trip with my family to Manhattan, home of some of my favorite FREAKS (see "Born-to-FREAK Heroes"), heroes like John Derian (decoupage artist), saucy Simon Doonan (writer and Creative Director at large for Barneys), and Bill Cunningham (street fashion photographer for *The New York Times*).

I hate to admit it, enlightened and madly skilled life coach that I am, but after paying airfare for six honey badgers (see "R is for RECKLESS DISREGARD"), I had expectations about how things would go. And not small expectations either, dagnabbit.

We checked into a family suite in a lovely hotel in Manhattan. How fabulous!

During the three minutes we rode the deceptively opulent mirror-encrusted elevator upwards, optimism reigned.

Then we walked into our "family suite," which turned out to be a room with two queen-size beds and a pullout couch. Only one person would be forced to sleep on the floor. I hastily tried to block out a flashback from a hotel stay a few months earlier involving lots of screaming. I began to fear another weekend-long KERFUFFLE.

Family suite or no, two adults and four kids living in one hotel room can be a depraved experience. There is no privacy. **To gain an advantage, be the first one through the door.** Almost immediately after landing, everyone has strewn the entire contents of their luggage on the floor, the beds, and any other surface in order to claim territory. Walking around a hotel room after we've landed in it can be hazardous to your health. It's not unlike the rhino outhouses of the wild, where spread-out piles of dung announce to other rhinos, **"I have been here and I won't be leaving anytime soon. Have a sniff. Deal with it."**

LANDING *An extremely rapid, informal process of staking a claim to personal territory in a new environment, involving activities and mental states not unlike during the Gold Rush and no less violent. The process of landing lasts approximately thirty seconds. After that, there's no property worth claiming that hasn't already been claimed.*

So, Rule Number One for sharing space in a hotel room with family: Claim your territory. Rule Number Two: Watch your step. If you don't, you may step into someone else's rhino kingdom. That's a dangerous move. (As is attempting a *coup d'état* on the remote control.)

So we all spread our dung, then we set out into the glorious city. Manhattan! (To paraphrase rapper Jay-Z: The city never sleeps. Somebody better slip me an Ambien.) Full of chic people to watch, fascinating places to explore, and glory to behold. Despite our adventure's primordial beginnings, I was determined to show these kids the magic of the Big Apple.

First stop: Central Park. It was a gloriously warm May day. My heart was bursting with elation and joy. Giant magnolia trees bloomed, birds sang, bees pollinated, amazing humans sauntered and strolled, pugs and poodles and French bulldogs of various shapes and colors roamed and sniffed. Bubbles were blown, street artists performed. How lucky we were! I experienced the kind of oneness only FREAKS can experience in such a cosmopolitan cosmos.

While the three younger kids chased each other up a huge rock and slid gleefully down on their behinds, George, age fourteen, who'd followed us from the hotel half a block behind, dragging his feet, turned to me and said darkly, "When can we go back to the hotel?" Oh dear Gawwwd, I thought, there could still be a KERFUFFLE brewing.

By the next afternoon, everyone's paws were barking, so all six of us boarded a tour bus. We could hop on and off the bus at various points of interest, which is a lovely way to see a city after you've hit the wall with hoofing it. It's especially great in Paris – except during a city-wide transportation strike, in which case, by all means, rent bicycles. But I digress (see "A is for ATTENTION DEFICIT").

It was a drizzly day. The kids decided to sit on the open top level of the bus and get rained on. Mark and I sat up in the drizzle, too, immediately behind the kids, to keep an eye on them. We were the only ones on top of the bus. Things started out innocently enough, but then the ancient rhinoceros energy began to rise. Even away from their staked-out territories in the hotel room, the kids started acting up – spitting at each other, shouting, wrestling – exactly like siblings on vacation together. Mark and I asked them nicely to settle down. Then we tried **The Gelato Bribe**. Then we got irate. It all put me and my dashing, enlightened husband in very bad moods.

RHINO REALITIES *To be fair, the rhinos I've observed in the wild were quite polite, keeping to themselves nicely unless they were caught off guard. Because they can't see very well, they sometimes get frightened by the world when they needn't have.*

After another five minutes of ineffectively watching the kids spitting on and punching each other, I had a strange yet brilliant idea: **Let's stop resisting this nonsense.** I'm a life coach, for Gawwwd's sake! I'd rather live in the solution, not the problem.

Mark and I simply moved to the back, away from the children, where we could keep an eye on them and ignore them (talented, aren't we?). From 25 feet away, we started having a much more pleasant experience.

I could have tried harder to thwart my children's shenanigans, but chose instead to take a vacation from my vacation problems. Yes, I was horrified to discover, when I went downstairs to escape the rain, that all the people on the lower level of the bus had heard everything. Yes, the bus driver reprimanded me and threatened to kick us all off if we didn't cut it out. All of that, yes, but when I made the decision to accept it all and take a vacation anyway, everything changed. **I became one with the whole experience and found peace within the KERFUFFLE.**

The next time your kids (or someone else's) or your family – or anyone, really – act like outrageous rhinos in the wild, ask yourself how good you're willing to let it get (see "U is for UPPER LIMIT"). Then decide to confound the KERFUFFLE by letting it be.

 How could you excuse yourself or get some distance (physically or metaphorically) from the KERFUFFLE?

IS FOR

LOVE

Though I crave speed and high velocity and getting EPIC stuff done in a flash, I've learned that most things worth creating take time, LOVE, and a big slab of patience. Typically, and unless you're God or Jebus, big, important things don't get done without assistance. And some may take a lifetime (or longer). **Knowing this helps me relax.**

JEBUS *Homer Simpson's version of God: "I can't be a missionary! I don't even believe in Jebus!"*

Consider the Taj Mahal. By rough estimation, creating it took 22 years, a thousand elephants, and over twenty thousand humans. **Imagine the physical force and power of one thousand majestic elephants.** And each of those twenty thousand humans had their own special talents. They were craftspeople, artisans, designers, architects, ditch diggers, lunch-makers ("Curry and naan, anyone?"), tree planters, carvers, supervisors, calligraphers, and accountants. There must have been umpteen setbacks, limitations, disasters, and failures along the way to completing the Taj Mahal: rain, cholera, chutney gone bad, general crankiness, and lots more.

Yet it got done.

The Taj was commissioned by grief-stricken Shah Jahan, in memory of his wife, Mumtaz Mahal, who died in childbirth. The Shah himself said this about the Taj:

"Should guilty seek asylum here,
Like one pardoned, he becomes free from sin.
Should a sinner make his way to this mansion,
All his past sins are to be washed away.
The sight of this mansion creates sorrowing sighs;
And the sun and the moon shed tears from their eyes."

The Shah created from LOVE. He dreamed that those who entered the Taj Mahal, that stunningly beautiful monument, might experience LOVE and cosmic pardoning. What an amazing intention! Perhaps in an effort to heal his own terrible pain, the Shah launched himself into a daunting project that would take up most of the rest of his life.

Get busy doing what
feels like love. Do it! NOW.

" *Alice*

When I think of the Taj Mahal, I think of its beauty and the inspiration behind it – the LOVE. When I'm working on projects that might take my lifetime – parenting my kids, contributing to my marriage, being a friend, doing my work as a coach and shamanic healer, and creating a body of work – I remember the burnt naan bread, exhausted people and elephants, and the long journey of completing the Taj Mahal. I remember that LOVE was why it was all envisioned in the first place.

When I know I'm going in my right direction, powered by a vision of LOVE, I think about who I want to take with me on the journey. The Shah didn't cook all those lunches on his own, and he surely didn't have the strength of a thousand elephants. Nor do I. **So who might have the skills to help me bring my own LOVE vision to life?** Who can help me get where I want to go? How can I begin? What do I need first?

Boredom is not an option. Remember why you loved this project in the first place. Goad yourself to action!

" *Alice*

I can begin without knowing what the final outcome will be. Perhaps what I create will be the Eighth Wonder of the World. If I'm motivated by LOVE, if my intentions come from LOVE, if this project is for LOVE ... well, then I can work and wait a lifetime for the results, because **beautiful things that matter take time.**

✲✲ What do you admire that's taken decades of attention or work to create?

✲✲ How can you use that example to inspire you when your born-to-FREAK self wants to hurry up and be done already?

✲✲ What pain have you experienced that you could use as inspiration for your own legacy of LOVE to the world?

Allow Myself to Introduce Myself

MAMA-SAN

MAMA-SAN

When our third child arrived, we moved into a much larger and grander home, in pursuit of bigger-and-better, and I began to feel trapped. I also began to have some sort of internal crisis of the soul, although I didn't really recognize it for that at first.

Our new home was lovely and gracious. It had acid-washed marble countertops and crystal chandeliers. We also had another place, a bohemian cabin at a lake in the woods. Dream life, right? The only trouble was that I was miserable. All the things I'd thought would make me happy really didn't.

For one thing, I was so dang exhausted all the time. After working ten-hour days at the hospital and spending the remaining six or seven waking hours caring for my brood (four fabulous kids by then, plus a husband and a dog), **the thought of "getting away" to our lake cabin sounded about as appealing as sticking a hot poker in my eye.**

I simply couldn't face The Cabin Get-Away Drill: pack everything and everyone up on Friday at five p.m. (after a nine-hour day at the hospital), drive to the cabin, then start cooking and cleaning all over again in a new location. At the cabin, in addition to cook and cleaner, my roles included lifeguard, s'mores-maker, laundress, Band-Aid applier, story reader, and day camp activity coordinator. Forty-three hours later, we'd leave the cabin and return home, where I'd unpack, make a big mess of everything, do more laundry, fall into bed, then get up and go back to work the next day.

I found it hard to disappoint my mother by not going to our cabin more often. She and my father had a cabin next door to ours, where they loved to spend time. My mom had been, during my childhood, a stay-at-home mom, and she didn't seem to understand why I wouldn't want to go up to the lake on the weekends. Because I wanted everyone's happiness, not just my own, I went through The Cabin Get-Away Drill more often than I really felt like I wanted to.

You may well ask how I got to that place of unconsciousness. **Have I mentioned that my husband is also a first-born overachiever, like I am?** We were both aces at pushing on through. In medical school, we'd learned that it's honorable to ignore physical and personal needs in order to get through whatever needs to be gotten through. So after medical school, we just kept pushing.

My mother wasn't the only person I disappointed. Whenever my kids got sick, my heart sank. Who should I let down this time? My kids or my partners at work? Whatever choice I made, I felt like I'd be letting myself down, too. Those were the toughest days. Some of my partners were none too happy if I chose to stay home with my sick kid, and they really disapproved when my kids started getting every virus known to humanity, as young kids in day care do.

Living that version of the fantastic modern woman's American Dream felt to me like being neither a good mom nor a good employee. And yet, apparently, *I had it all.*

My life had become ridiculously complicated. What I'd previously been able to handle – going to work and hyper-lock focusing on my slides, giving a hundred percent at work when I was there – was getting more and more impossible to achieve. As the things I valued – love, connection, my children and family, playfulness, and irreverence – seemed to drain out of my life, my spirit began to feel more and more crushed.

Never stop chasing after love.
Even if the po-po are on your tail.
Even then.

" *Alice*

The earth I believed to be solid beneath my feet began to shift. I could no longer maintain the balance I'd previously and contentedly experienced in the arms of my medical career. I **missed mothering, cooking, creating, puttering, and simply being.** Looking back on my own childhood, I realized that being a mom was what I'd most wanted to be. I adored caring for all living things and as a kid had spent almost every free moment training to be a babysitter and then being one for so many lovely families and kids.

During that crazy time when my soul was slipping away, my husband Mark and I often laughed (darkly) about how we used to be *interesting* and have *passions and dreams*. We'd mostly forgotten about them, having filled our heads instead with knowledge and filled our lives with so much stuff that there was no room left for what we considered essential.

Our fourth child, Charlie, was one of those kids who came into this world to show others what love is. One day, at the Department of Motor Vehicles office, where I'd gone to renew my driver's license, I ran into an old friend – a sports trainer at a university. When Charlie toddled over to meet my friend and look him in the eye, my friend spontaneously burst into tears!

Charlie's presence was (and is) so loving and powerful. My friend looked at me with tears streaming down his face and said, "Wow, he really is something special." "Yes," I said, "I know."

Snuggle together.
Recharge at the base station.

" *Alice*

Something in me shifted that day, too. I realized I was ready to relish and enjoy our kids – **the magical and wondrous creatures who'd come into our lives** – to lavish them with love, bake for them, read to them, take them on adventures to the beach, to the movies, to the grocery store, snuggle with them and watch nature documentaries. I eventually did do all of those things with them, and more, but back then **I had little left to give after working all day.** And that made me sad.

I was also desperate for entertainment and a social life. I wanted to have fun. So I often threw large parties at our house. That might seem contradictory, considering everything I've just said, but I loved throwing those parties and seemed to have endless energy for it. Looking back, I think I found that energy because socializing fed my soul.

In the evenings, I was like a twisted hybrid of Martha Stewart and Julie McCoy (the Social Director on *The Love Boat*). I so desperately needed my fix of fun in order to be able to soldier on at my day job. I knew my parties were feeding others' souls, too, because at the ends of those nights, we'd all be grinning from ear to ear, telling each other we were so grateful to be in each other's presence, and already planning our next get-together.

In the end, thankfully, my inner mother won out. As convoluted and odd as it turned out to be, I found a way to reclaim the joy of being with my children and being with myself. I'm so thrilled to see how happy my kids are and how happy I am after reclaiming my role as mother again.

My children often call me **mama-san**, which I always thought was a nice Japanese term for **mother**. Today I learned that it actually means something more like **night club supervisor** – not an appropriate Japanese term for a mother at all!

And yet ...

Words are funny and fascinating, aren't they? When I really think it through, I realize that I relish both my *mother* role and my *mama-san* role. **I am mother of several and mama-san nurturer of many.** That feels just right to me.

To become a mama-san of many – creative social director, life coach, author, and goader – I first had to mother myself.

Commit to believing you deserve to experience all the love and connection your heart desires. No earning or repenting or serving time is required. (Elephants never forget this.)

" *Alice*

M IS FOR

MEA CULPA

When my son George was eleven, a friend invited him to football camp. "Sure," George said in an upbeat yet noncommittal way, which I learned (years later) to interpret as "There's no way in hell I'm doing that." I took George at his word (vs. his soul's vernacular), phoned up his friend's mom (a dear friend of mine), and we signed our boys up for football camp. **Mayhem ensued.**

May I begin by saying **MEA CULPA** ("my mistake"). I am human, and bound to make mistakes.

Our born-to-FREAK brains are hard-wired to take in a lot of data simultaneously, synthesize it, and improvise fantastic solutions (yay!), but I've found that the various kinds of noise four kids make can quickly become overwhelming if I'm not centered and at peace.

We FREAKS do best when we operate from the quiet center of the self. We can also be so full of love and empathy (see "W is for WHY AM I CONCERNED?") that it's difficult to separate ourselves from others and find what's best for each, or all, including ourselves. **We're sometimes faced with difficult choices, required to make decisions in a red-hot moment.** And sometimes things don't work out so well.

Fast-forward eight weeks. **It all goes down during the morning commute.** I wake the kids at 6:30, pack a few tiny backpacks, and attempt to get everyone into the car and off to day care, preschool, and (oh, God, here it comes) football camp. I'm rushed. I'm not at my best. I'm not centered.

Before he gets into the van, I remind George what's on his schedule for today. He darts his big brown eyes at me fearfully, then runs like a bat out of hell into the yard, muttering **"I am NOT going."** Uh-oh. I sense I'm about to experience extreme difficulty.

I run after George and tackle him. Yes, really, but as gently and maternally as possible. Then I sort of wrestle him into the van. (The neighbors could probably give a full report. I've blocked out the details.) Motherhood is sometimes a full-contact sport.

After dropping the other kids off, I barrel down tree-lined streets toward George's friend's house. From the back of the van, George says again, simply and quietly, "I am not going." Shit. Panic and fear set in.

I can hear my mother's voice urging me to follow through on all commitments ("He can quit after football camp is over."). It doesn't seem nice of George to bail out on his friend now, leaving him to face football camp alone. And my pager has already gone off once. The pressures are building. I'm already overwhelmed, and George isn't helping. In no way am I operating from my quiet center.

As we pull into our friends' driveway, I drag my weary, scrubs-wearing self out of the van. **I prepare to be effervescent and sparkling as I head to the front door to exchange niceties** before I drive to work. But George isn't behind me. I turn in time to see him bolt out of the van and disappear around the side of the house.

We stare out the kitchen window into the rather large backyard until my friend's husband, who has a good eye for fugitives, points and says, "Isn't that him there, in the bushes?" Yep. **There's George, crouching in the bushes, attempting to disappear into the forest floor.** He sees that his cover has been blown and changes tactics, loping across the yard with a badly improvised fake limp to ensure that we see the obvious: Attending football camp with such a grievous injury isn't even a remote possibility.

In such moments, being born to FREAK really blows. On the one hand, I want to be tough, but on the other hand, I just want to pull my kid onto my lap and hold him as we weep together uncontrollably. My friend's salty eighty-year-old mother shrugs and says, "If he doesn't want to go, don't make him." That resonates. A lot. I begin to feel a little more centered.

I drop George off at his usual, non-football day camp and wonder what parent in good conscience could ever force a kid to do something that terrified him that much. I discover the answer to that question in about 39 seconds.

Transitions are not necessarily your forte. Explaining your propensity to be abrupt can smooth things over with non-FREAKS.

" *Alice*

As I speed toward the hospital to check in for work, my husband Mark calls and I tell him what has just transpired – the refusal, the escape, the reconciliation. His response is, **"You let him get away with THAT!??"** I immediately feel judged. My blood boils. I tell Mark that if he's so disappointed in my performance, maybe he should leave work at noon (pretty much impossible for him) and take George to football camp himself. Mark's response is a quiet "Fine." I've just thrown George, a scared eleven-year-old, under the bus of an ambush by his dad.

I arrive at work exhausted, sad (about the tackling and about getting mad at my husband), and smiling (at the backyard showdown). If I look at it all from high above, it's actually rawwwther funny. But I have a hundred slides to read and a pile-up of beeper pages to answer, so I get to work.

MEA CULPA.

When I viewed it all with hindsight, I wished I'd heard and accepted George's refusal to go to football camp, even though it was a late reveal. I could have supported him to follow his inner guidance. We could have wiped our brows and gone peacefully on our way. And I wished I hadn't gotten angry at my husband. As soon as I realized all of that, I apologized to them both.

I've learned that MEA CULPA is a very powerful and healing concept for FREAKS: "My mistake." "I'm at fault." "Yes, I am imperfect," followed pretty quickly by "I love you. Please forgive me."

When I get off track or when I'm not centered and I react to my kids in a way that doesn't feel good, I apologize to them. It helps keep things clear between us. And they get to see that **I know how it went down and I'm willing to take responsibility for what's mine.** Maybe my role-modeling of MEA CULPA will pay off in their own lives.

Despite all the yoga, yogurt, self-awareness, affirmations, herbal tea, and great intentions, there will always be times when we blunder mightily – in our judgments, through our actions, with our words, with ourselves, our children, friends, co-workers, and lovers. **MEA CULPA can help us get back on track.** From a place of recognizing and acknowledging when we're at fault, we can apologize to whoever we've harmed and begin again with the intention of spreading loving kindness as we go about our lives.

Let your defects shine.
They're what make you so fucking kick-ass.

I invite all FREAKS to apply self-compassion when we've erred. Whaling on ourselves mercilessly after the situation's expiry date doesn't help anyone. Acknowledge your part and apologize: "MEA CULPA." Then drop it like a hot potato. You have EPIC things to do.

✸✸ If you've contributed to a problem or drama or situation that's not great, how can you take responsibility for your part in it? Who do you need to say "MEA CULPA" to and how do you want to say it?

✸✸ How can you carve out a little time at the beginning of your day to tune in to your quiet center and set your intentions so the day is easier and so you're easier on yourself?

IS FOR

NOTORIOUS

"Forget safety.

Live where you fear to live.

Destroy your reputation.

Be notorious."

– Rumi

It can be dangerous to be who you really are, especially if it threatens what's "acceptable." **Currently and historically, we who were born to FREAK are often pathologized** – labeled as having an element that must be eliminated or normalized. Those who crave order and rules (those not born to FREAK) seek to fit people and things into neat boxes. Being NOTORIOUS may mean being famous for all the wrong reasons in some people's eyes, but we who were born to FREAK must absolutely learn to feel good about it.

Thank goodness we FREAKS have dared to be NOTORIOUS in our own unique ways. **FREAKS have made amazing contributions to humanity.** Think of FREAK heroes like Gandhi, Anne Lamott, Martha Beck, Nelson Mandela, Mother Teresa, Steve Martin, Oprah, Tina Fey, Temple Grandin, Jesus, Johnny Depp, Lady Gaga, David Sedaris, and Stephen Colbert – all people who saw how things could be different and made it happen in the world, in many cases making great sacrifices in the process.

Fear is a funny thing. Through my work with humans and Beasties, I've learned that some Beasties are NOTORIOUS, too – like sharks, venomous snakes, wolves, and black widow spiders. They've become NOTORIOUS because of their power. They're feared. And they have much to teach us (see "B is for BLACK MAMBA").

BEASTIES *For more about connecting with Beastie energies and tapping into their guidance and empowerment, see my book* What The Walrus Knows.

As I've learned more about NOTORIOUS Beasties that scared the bejesus out of me, I've calmed down – because I've been stunned by the beauty of what I've learned about them and through them. **Majestic, NOTORIOUS Beasties are simply doing what they were designed to do.** They follow their natural desires. Without holding back. Without apology. Maybe that's why they scare us so much.

I see NOTORIOUS Beasties differently now. Mind you, I don't invite venomous snakes and sharks into my living room, but learning about them has made me wonder ... What if we went about our lives without holding back? What if we went after our desires without apology, like a great white shark rockets after its prey, with powerful directness and conviction, even if it means we become NOTORIOUS?

Get all extinct and mythical.
When you're feeling it.

 " *Alice*

Go confidently. **Go as your true self.** Like the powerful and NOTORIOUS Beasties we humans revere and sometimes fear, you were born to FREAK. **So FREAK.**

 What would you do if you didn't fear your reputation being destroyed?

 If you were completely and totally yourself, what would you be NOTORIOUS for ?

O IS FOR

OFF-LEASH

In the wilds of a blizzard-ridden country, a nutty-cakes sled-dog guy who kept his dogs chained up in spite of their incessant barks (which were, I'm convinced, desperate cries for freedom from him) told me I should never, under any circumstances, let my dog run OFF-LEASH, as so many dangers could befall her. Like what? **Skunk ambushes or ninja deer**, I suppose. He was really trying to unfluence me.

> **UNFLUENCE** *When someone is a negative influence on you, wanting to dissuade you from what you know in your heart is true for you.*

When people pull me over to the curb to warn me about the dangers of something – like quitting my job or surfing or sharks or keeping my children in public school – that's always a good time to check in with myself. **Is what I consider the right thing to do actually, REALLY dangerous?** If it truly does all of a sudden feel dangerous, I may decide to stop. Often, though, after checking in with myself, I realize that the fears in question belong to the warner (them), not the warnee (me). The fears being waved around are more about what they fear than what

I fear. It's often mostly not about me at all.

**Tear your stake from the ground.
Gallop from idea to idea.**

" *Alice*

As much as I love my precious Spirit Francis the Wonder Dog, I could never keep her leashed 24/7. She has an inner lawless spirit that must be freed daily, despite the devilish perils of the wild forest. **Dark-hearted squirrels lurk in wait to taunt** her, but that never stops her. She revels in being free.

Being free is not just for Catholic dogs with strong herding instincts. **All FREAKS need OFF-LEASH time in wild places of some type** (whether actual or metaphorical), where we can be completely untamed and allowed to explore whatever our hearts desire. Sniffing. Examining things. Following our curiosity. Meeting new beings. It's imperative to support our own FREAKINESS in this way.

**Find ways to feel WILD and ALIVE that
aren't destructive to body, mind,
pocketbook, or living beings.**

" *Alice*

Being leashed is fine during some parts of the day. After all, I do have four kids to raise, meals to make, and bills to pay. But I can much more passionately dedicate myself to carpooling, bathing, grocery shopping, and bed-tucking (and I can behave myself better), if I've **roamed unfettered and unrestrained** for a while. Every day. Preferably before I start working in the morning.

When was the last time you got to be OFF-LEASH?

In what ways do you like to be OFF-LEASH?

What do you like to bound over to and sniff when you're OFF-LEASH?

Find a hole in the fence.
Let yourself run wild and free at
least thirty minutes a day.

" *Alice*

CREATIVE DIRECTOR EXTRAORDINAIRE

In photos of me at age three, I have a mad cap of wild, woolly hair that blows crazily in the wind, untouched by humans or grooming instruments. My mother says it was so awful to brush my hair (I would cry and cry) that she couldn't stand to do it.

There's still a three-year-old part of me that's happiest and feels most beautiful when ungroomed, unmade-up, and wandering in the woods or just hanging with friends. Sometimes, love is ... never having to blow-dry. I still pout at the thought of having to go for a haircut and will do just about anything to avoid it.

According to all reports, I refused to allow anyone to dress me, preferring to choose outfits for myself that didn't match, at least not conventionally. "In what way did they not match?" I can't help but ask now. They matched just fine to me. **Thank goodness my mother indulged me (perhaps she was too tired to argue).**

The way we dress is one of the wonderful ways we express ourselves. I still enjoy wearing combinations of stripes and leopard prints and coming up with outfits that cause non-FREAKS to say, with bugged-out eyes, "Wow. That's quite a combination." Yes, it is, thank you, and it pleases me immensely.

Despite my ungroomable bohemian nature (or maybe because of it), I've realized that I'm a CREATIVE DIRECTOR. Being a CREATIVE DIRECTOR is really about envisioning ways of expressing intangibles – ideas, feelings, and moods – with materials. I have moods I want to convey and ideas I want to express so that I and others can see them. I love using clothes and costume jewelry when I want to make an impression or create a mood or get "balls-to-the-wall pretty," as my sister calls it. The more I allow myself the freedom to wear whatever I want, the better I feel.

The lack of rules about dressing as I was growing up helped me discover my role as CREATIVE DIRECTOR. FREAKS need a lot of room to explore and play in order to be infinitely creative. Finding an outfit that creates a positive physical reaction inside feels fantastic. Fellow freak and fashion icon Iris Apfel calls this a *bolt of lightning*:

> "I look at a piece of fabric and listen to the threads.
> It tells me a story. It sings me a song.
> I have to get a physical reaction when I buy something.
> A Coup de Foudre – a bolt of lightning.
> It's fun to get knocked out that way!"
>
> – Iris Apfel

FREAKS seem to have an ability to sense and feel the effects of shoes, necklaces, suits, and hats (and slipcovers and vases and lots of other tangible goods). **By creating a wardrobe and wearing outfits that vibrate on the same frequency I do, I get to feel pretty amazing.** When we FREAKS feel great in what we're wearing, we can raise the vibe of everyone we connect with. Beauty and style can speak to and uplift others. Seeing someone in a fantastic outfit can alter my day.

Examine beauty often. Eat with your eyes.
It buoys you up. Do it daily.

" *Alice*

Over time, I've learned that I'm suited to the role of visionary – one who imagines what can be. I'm in a near-constant state of using my feelings to edit, eliminate, and collect interesting elements for creating my wardrobe and my home.

Being a CREATIVE DIRECTOR keeps me jazzed for my life's true work of envisioning possibilities for healing and inspiring myself and others.

 IS FOR

PACHYDERMAL PATIENCE

Many of us who were born to FREAK have been told to be patient, to slow down, simmer down, and pipe down so many times it may have left us feeling as if something's wrong with us. Our trigger-happy, risk-taking impulsiveness, which can serve us so well in creative adventures and in life in general, also has a dark side: impatience. **As much as I've resisted being patient my whole life, I've also learned a lot about this virtue and its benefits.** Especially from elephants.

I once watched a PBS documentary (*Echo: An Elephant to Remember*) about an elephant matriarch. The film is really like a marvelous wake for Echo, an amazing elephant who'd graced the Earth for 65 years with her wonderful pachydermal presence. The documentary chronicles many dramatic stories of her life, but one story in particular stood out for me in its quivering, elephantine beauty.

Echo, attended by both her sister and her eldest daughter, gave birth to a baby. When a freshly hatched elephant arrives, it has one big job to do. It must get into a standing position so it can reach its mother's teat and take in much-needed nourishment and hydration. The African savannah is an unforgiving place and baby elephants who don't stand within a few hours ordinarily perish.

This baby struggled from the get-go. Despite trying and trying, it seemed unable to stand. The film crew began to sense doom and questioned whether they even wanted to go on filming, as it became terribly unlikely that the baby would make it. The rest of the elephant herd moved on to search for water, leaving the three lady elephants and the baby behind.

Echo tirelessly supported and encouraged her baby, lifting him up, nudging him, trying to ease him into position for success. The baby's auntie and sister stayed valiantly at Echo's side, supporting with their presence, with touches and looks, pitching in when they had the opportunity. It was absolutely heartbreaking to watch.

Never, ever give up hope.
Reach out for a hand up.
Find a fellow FREAK to lift you up,
as you've lifted so many others.

" Alice

An hour passed, then two hours, then twelve hours — way beyond the accepted normal amount of time for a new calf to be able to successfully stand. Then something weird happened. Despite his exhaustion, despite the lack of liquids, despite the beating sun, **the baby somehow gathered up one hind leg, and then the other, and, in one glorious final heave-ho, stood up!** And stayed up. The joy at the scene was palpable, evident in the elephants themselves and heard in the voices of the film crew.

That incredible, life-sustaining miracle was only possible through love and PACHYDERMAL PATIENCE. I'm guessing the elephantine expectations of Echo for her baby made the miracle possible.

> Even elephants (as awe-inspiring
> and amazing as we are) always remember
> that we're part of a herd.
>
> " *Alice*

How amazing it is when we offer sustained PACHYDERMAL PATIENCE like Echo's to our own clumsy selves as we trod our paths, to our children, to our spouses and friends and clients. When we're positively pachydermal – nudging, cheering, choosing love over and over again, praying softly (to whomever we pray), and simply being present – we can expect miracles.

❀❀ What or who would you like to offer PACHYDERMAL PATIENCE to – out of love and dreaming of a miracle?

❀❀ If you gave yourself PACHYDERMAL PATIENCE, what in your life or inside of you might heave-ho to an upright position in victory?

IS FOR

QUEERS

There's something so wondrous, fun, incredibly courageous, and utterly honest about gay people who are out and completely, splendidly who they are in a world where it can be perilous to be a QUEER. Being a FREAK is not easy in these dark times. It can even be downright dangerous. And yet, here are these wonderful humans, being so luminous and beautiful about who they truly are. They defy the rules. They dare to live betwixt and between genders, unbound by strict definitions.

Stop giving a rat's patootie about whether others understand, accept, or celebrate your creative endeavors.

Create daily in your favorite mediums.

" *Alice*

I've learned that in indigenous societies around the planet, people who blurred the gender lines were considered "two-spirited," embodying both masculine and feminine spirits, defying gender characterization in a way that's neither nor.

sarah bamford seidelmann m.d. | www.borntoFREAK.com

They were not only accepted, but highly revered. Two-spirited men and women were often consulted about important issues. In many cases, they were feared, as they were believed to be full of power – power in the shamanic sense of being chosen by the spirits. They were considered to be gifted with universe-bending power.

In the vast majority of traditional cultures, there were no hard and fast rules about two-spirited people. **For example, two-spirited males did typically female work at times and at other times they did typically male work.** Two-spirited people were artisans who created ceremonial dress (fashion!), healers, shamans, singers, and dancers, often performing both traditionally masculine and traditionally feminine roles. **They blurred the lines.** To try to describe or delimit what they did would be impossible because they were as unique and uncategorizable as every FREAK is.

The key point I'm making here is that **two-spirited people were needed. They were celebrated.** They were revered for their unique talents. Wouldn't it be great to see our current culture embrace and celebrate the uniqueness of all individuals, including QUEERS?

I love it that people are gay, lesbian, transgender, bisexual, or whatever they are. A unique but not easily categorized or understood person is special, chosen by the universe (or spirit or God) to bring balance to their community, to serve in roles that would otherwise go unfilled, to FREAK, so that the entire community thrives as a whole ... because **everyone has a place in the whole.**

The many two-spirited people I've had the pleasure of knowing and admiring in my life have been among some of the most beautiful, courageous, open-hearted, powerful, hilarious, and healing people I've met. **It's as if their very being, as it challenges and defies categorization, brings balance to the world.**

As a fellow FREAK, I celebrate the two-spirited ones, like Jim Henson and his gift of Muppets, Tim Gunn (*Project Runway*), Martha Beck (*Finding Your Own North Star*), Ellen DeGeneres, Jane Lynch of *Glee*, Carson Kressley (*Queer Eye for the Straight Guy*), Elton John, David Sedaris (*Me Talk Pretty One Day*), Simon Doonan (*Eccentric Glamour*), and Freddie Mercury of the band Queen, to name only a few.

For those of us who were born to FREAK, QUEERS are often some of the very best role models, fearlessly sharing who they are without explanation, justification, or apology.

 Even if you're not a QUEER or other two-spirited being, how can you embrace the betwixt-and-between places that would bring you more into balance?

 How could you safely and unapologetically bring more aspects of your true self out into the world, even if that's a bit scary?

 IS FOR

RECKLESS DISREGARD

Regardless of what difficulties or challenges we face in life, I find that it's powerful and fantastic to have a RECKLESS DISREGARD for what other people think, especially for us FREAKS.

By design, many of us FREAKS will have lives that are not typical. We'll make unique choices that may seem radical to others. Having a RECKLESS DISREGARD for others' opinions is what radical self-love looks like. Giving up your concerns about what other people think allows you to discover unique solutions for your own personal suffering. **Truly, there's very little else that needs to be done other than loving yourself radically in this way.**

```
    Point your beak in a different direction.
          Ignore all the other birds.
```

" Alice

RECKLESS DISREGARD is particularly important when making big, bold moves that come from a true heart's desire – embarking on a new adventure, leaving a job, going back to school, ending a marriage, publishing those poems. As in any new adventure, there can be moments of doubt. Naysayers may show up. But, **deep down in your core, when you're quiet and still, you can sense the perfect choice for you. You have a *knowing*.**

In my own life, I discovered that without truly embracing the concept of RECKLESS DISREGARD, **it's not easy to quit being a doctor in order to intensely study animal totems.** As I was leaving my physician's job, I bumped into a colleague who told me I was a fool to leave. **She said I didn't know what I was doing and I would regret it.** She said I could lose all my financial security. Whoa! It was hard-core to hear all of that coming from someone I really liked and respected … but I carried on, regardless.

I've learned the lesson of radical self-love and RECKLESS DISREGARD over time, by observing wild animals. **Wild animals aren't caught up in their heads, trying to save face, keep up with the Joneses, or tow the line.** They're simply tuned in to their instincts, doing whatever they need to do next to care for themselves, their families, and what's most important to them.

One Beastie in particular has taught me about RECKLESS DISREGARD: the honey badger. The honey badger, it turns out, is the most audacious animal ever. There's a hilarious YouTube video that's a rawwwther salty and irreverent spoof of a serious BBC nature documentary about the honey badger. It's called *The Crazy Nastyass Honey Badger* and shows a real honey badger going about its business — which includes many seemingly dangerous tasks, such as diving into caves stuffed with stinging bees to eat their larvae and biting the heads off

sarah bamford seidelmann m.d. | www.borntoFREAK.com

of vipers in treetops. The video's comedic narrator says the honey badger simply "doesn't give a shit" what anyone thinks of him.

Be INTENSE. Step lively.
Embrace your inner honey badger.

" *Alice*

It's plain to see that the honey badger* is entirely comfortable doing all of those intense activities. He appears to truly be at ease and enjoying life. **Well, occasionally, he does get bitten by vipers and so must sleep off the resulting venom-induced sedation,** but afterwards he gets up and goes right back to doing what he loves. He's simply following his instincts to take care of his own needs and desires.

The surprising rant from my colleague when I left my job came at a time when I was still a bit hesitant about my decision to leave. **Was I making a mistake?** Maybe. **Did I feel entirely sure about where my new choice would take me?** Hell, no. Could I still turn back? Yes. **Did I want to?** ... Well, no, actually. With every fiber of my being, I could feel that I was supposed to do what I was planning to do.

Zoom past the poor sods waiting to do
things perfectly. Do it however you do it.
Elephants (and FREAKS) are like that.

" *Alice*

Whenever I begin to worry about what others think of the paths I choose to take or what I'm up to – professionally, personally, parentally – it always helps me to remember the honey badger. **I just keep plunging in with RECKLESS DISREGARD for the opinions of others**, going after what my heart desires. After all, who else but me can know what's best for me?

Who else but you can know what's best for you?

 What does your heart desire now?

 How could you pursue that with a RECKLESS DISREGARD for the opinions of others?

If you had a RECKLESS DISREGARD for the opinions of others, what would you want to change about your life, your work, your family life, or your social life?

* For more about animals and animal totems (including a "Honey Badger Manifesto"), see my book What the Walrus Knows.

IS FOR

SURFING

SURFING is a particularly relevant sport for us who were born to FREAK. It's an intense physical endeavor, helping expend the voracious extra energy coursing through our bodies. And it's a boatload of fun. **FREAKS need fun like non-freaks need to file things.** Our minds are liquid. The ocean is our friend.

From the first moment, SURFING slays the ego. If you think you're the master of the waves (or the world), when you SURF you'll quickly and unpleasantly realize that, instead, those waves own you. Humility is very important for FREAKS to foster. People born to FREAK can head into the dangerous territory of thinking they (and they alone) are divine. We often live in the thin place between the ordinary and the otherworldly, and so many crazy, magical things happen to us (or within us) that sometimes we begin to think we're alone in that. Thankfully, we're not.

Ubuntu is a very useful concept. *Ubuntu* is the Zulu/Xhosa word for the philosophy of *I am because we are*, as in, *I SURF because the ocean exists. If I'm lucky and respectful and focused and intentional, the ocean will let me ride on its lovely waves that are packed with power and energy and oodles of fun. Or maybe today is not my day for this.* I think the ocean likes it when we show that we're filled with humility and willing to surrender. The ocean is probably laughing as it takes us all the way in to shore.

```
People, what are you waiting for?
The fantastic (metaphorical) waves keep
rolling on in. Why not jump on one and
start to SURF? The best SURFER is
the one having the most F U N!
```

 " *Alice*

I came to SURFING at the age of 44. The first time I paddled out to where the waves were breaking it felt a teensy, weensy bit terrifying. Thank goodness my dear friend Susan was leading me, as she's strong and courageous. I figured she'd kick any shark's or rogue wave's ass if they tried to hurt me. I put my head down on my longboard and began moving through the water with big arm strokes. I felt a lot better when we arrived at our not-so-secret spot and I saw a boatload of three-year-olds already there, catching waves with their groovy, stoked parents, and also a mess of 55-plus-year-old dudes who looked like they were already missing their briefcases and boardrooms. The dudes stared with genuine concern at the water, watching **the teeny eight-inch-high wave sets roll in. The scene that day was a good example of how SURFING equalizes us all.**

I got into position, as Susan had taught me, and waited for waves. When I saw a decent wave, I heaved my carcass onto the board and then, as instructed, paddled like a bat out of hell … and still missed the wave. Mercifully, Susan pushed me onto the next wave. This time it felt different. Instead of feeling the wave sink and crumble beneath me, all of a sudden I felt a huge surge of power push right up under me. I stopped paddling and hurtled along with no effort at all. Then I leaped up into my karate stance, and there I was! – flying along on top of the water, incredibly giddy with glee. When the wave petered out and I flopped into the water, I couldn't wait to get back in line to go catch another one.

Over the next six days, I SURFED and tried to SURF on many, many waves. **I went at it like I had a crack addiction, only it was a SURFING addiction, and healthy.** Well, maybe a little bit harmful. My leg and hip got so badly bruised from slamming myself onto the board like a crazed zealot that I looked a bit of a wreck. I could not have cared less. At night, my body hurt to the point where I rolled around in bed and moaned. **"Sweet Jebus, please can't we have a day off?"** But in the morning, I'd pop up out of bed, hobble toward coffee and a green smoothie, and after a brief and awkward Sun Salutation, haul my large, hot-waxed surfboard into the water yet again, eager to jazz the glass (ride waves).

On the second day, I noticed it was more difficult to catch a wave. I think beginner's luck has something to do with nonattachment. On the first day, I didn't know if I'd ever be able to catch a wave. I was just in a space of being willing. By the second day, when I knew what it felt like to catch a wave, I had full-on wave greed. I wanted to catch all the waves. When I tried, my paddling arms got exhausted.

Luckily, Susan, the fearless conqueror, introduced me to Bill Hamilton – fabulous human, legendary surfboard shaper, and stepfather of famous surfer Laird Hamilton. He watched me for a bit, then explained my problem to me. He said, **"Sarah, you gotta cherry pick 'em. You're paddling out to too many**

waves." He told me to be patient and wait for the cherry to grow on the tree, and only pick the cherries that are ripe and sweet.

Sure enough, things improved as I began to wait for waves that looked ideal, though I developed my own analogy for what to look for. **Ideal waves seemed crispy fried, like they had a bit of crackle to them.** If I got into position in time, I often caught them and ... oh man, what a feeling it was to fly along being SURFED by the ocean after having been pounded for a while.

Stay nice and loosey, goosey.

" *Alice*

What a great and useful metaphor this is for those born to FREAK: Wait for the best wave, the one that's ready and ripe for the picking (or crispy fried to a crackly crunch). In doing so, we avoid scattering our creative energy, reserving it for waves that offer us the best opportunities. You may not catch every opportunity you paddle out to, but saving your strength for the crispy, delicious ones sure increases your chance of success.

If you decide you want the wave that's caught your eye, you've got to paddle out to it. You've got to intend to merge with it, knowing it might not work out, knowing there might be a fall. **Because if you do connect with that opportunity, you'll get to experience the *Ubuntu* of it.** You'll get to influence and be influenced by it. You'll get to frolic in that effortless place where you're catapulted forward by mysterious forces that are larger than you.

If you don't paddle out, you won't get the experience. So take the risk. Give yourself the chance to ride a glorious wave.

Check out some of the waves on your horizon. Which ones are worthy? Which ones make you want to paddle out hard and fast (like Gloria Steinem scooting out of Hooters)?

Allow Myself to Introduce Myself

INDOCTRINATOR

INDOCTRINATOR

As we were growing up, my younger sister and only sibling, Maria, seemed to me to be a terribly delicate, emotional, and easily affected flower of a human being. She wasn't totally unlike me, yet I, perhaps in error, instinctively sensed or believed that I was stronger – and not just because I was older. She seemed so very sensitive and vulnerable. It concerned me that if Maria ever attempted to leave the house, the world would surely eat her alive. So I took it upon myself to harden her, through my own odd boot camp, which I created out of my love for her.

Training Maria consisted of doing things like **teaching her to say bad four-letter words, showing her how to do naughty things, and tying her to the bedposts with socks.** In my version, the socks were barely tied at all – tied so loosely she could have easily escaped by herself. In the victim's ... I mean my sister's version, she was unable to free herself and so was left tied up alone for hours. **(May I remind us all here that there is no reality, only perception.)** Perhaps, in doing things like making Maria say bad four-letter words, I simply wanted her to also get into a bit of trouble, to take the focus off of me!

Some of the most terrible deeds we do, we do out of love, until we know better. My parents didn't see my antics with Maria as being positive or loving. They told me I was being "unkind, cruel, and too much." I began to realize that my efforts in helping the world at large were not always welcome. My response was to go undercover with my training programs, meaning that I'd continue doing them, but without being found out. Though I knew I couldn't let my parents catch me, it was still imperative to toughen Maria up before the world harmed her or swallowed her up. I had to do it. I loved her that much.

I've since seen my own kids do the same dance with each other. I've seen our oldest trying to squelch out behavior and mannerisms in the younger kids which might be perceived as weak, odd, unappealing, or inappropriate by classmates at school.

While we discourage the squelching of anyone's authentic self at our house, I find that I can **sympathize with both the trainee and the drill sergeant** ... (ahem) I mean indoctrinator.

My inclination to be a self-appointed indoctrinator didn't stop at home. I single-handedly took on the role of sex instructor with my friends in third grade, because I found reproduction fascinating and considered it a crying shame not to share such important life details. **The sex information I had was top-notch**, as it came directly from my mother and included lots of technical jargon, like *penis* and *vagina,* which seemed to satisfy my classmates. An odd result of my informal sex education activities was that some of my classmates' parents seemed relieved, like maybe they hadn't felt up to the task themselves and, for some reason (?!), they trusted me to do it.

I no longer share bodies of knowledge without being asked to, with one exception: my kids. But even with them, I try to wait until I'm asked. I've learned my lesson about toughening people up or squelching sensitive natures, because I know now (and have for a long time) that such qualities are to be fostered and celebrated.

T IS FOR

THAT BRINGS UP MY SHIT

I just got back from Jazz The Glass, a surfing and shamanism retreat in Hawaii that I co-created for women who were born to FREAK. As often happens when FREAKS gather together, **it was a stunning, fantastic, deep, and wondrous experience.**

One of the things I marveled at was how many people came to the retreat not because surfing sounded fun or because studying shamanism might be sort of interesting. Many of the participants showed up, consciously or unconsciously, to see what would happen if they did something that scared them, **something that really BROUGHT UP THEIR SHIT**. Mind you, we were no ordinary gang of females. We were a bunch of courageous honey badgers (see "R is for RECKLESS DISREGARD"), willing to push the envelope of life to see what we might discover about ourselves.

To be frank, it BRINGS UP MY SHIT to go traveling with a group of women I don't know very well. And especially to go as their leader. Even though I'd led that kind of trip before, there was an uneasy part of me wondering what might unfold. **I was facing**

the great unknown: Did I have the skills I'd need? Would people get along? Would they be happy with what we'd planned?

Anyone who's traveled or shared a house with strangers knows there's the potential for it to be like **the worst kind of group tent camping in very bad weather**. And even when we're with people we already know, traveling to foreign places can really BRING UP OUR SHIT. I prepared as much as humanly possible, then flew to Hawaii.

Susan, my surfer co-leader (who'd also just flown in), and I went to the bay to examine our beloved waves, the ones that had carried us so delightfully to shore during last summer's inaugural retreat. **But wait. What??** The entire shape of the waves had changed, and there were no waves in our "secret spot." In fact, the beach was all wonky. It looked like it had been heaved up and tossed around by an irritated Mother Earth. **Hells bells.** That BROUGHT UP SUSAN'S SHIT, as she was the go-to gal in charge of all things surf. It also BROUGHT UP MY SHIT, as the retreat co-leader. I tried to help by remaining untroubled.

> **U**NTROUBLED *"Troubled? Then stay with me, for I am not." – Hāfez*
>
> *Remaining untroubled when others are troubled keeps us from adding trouble onto trouble. Who needs double the trouble? To me, being untroubled – remaining at peace, not anxious – is pretty much the most awesome thing in the world I can be. I don't hit that mark a hundred percent of the time, but it's what I shoot for 24/7.*

Susan looked around in confusion for a while, searching the horizon for what had become of the waves we longed for. Then she looked dismayed and upset. Susan is a walking ball of sunshine, and I'd rarely seen her that upset. **Yes, her shit had most definitely been brought up.** What will we do if there are no waves? What if the only waves are out where it's deep and that BRINGS UP EVERYONE'S SHIT? What if everyone gets mad?

The thing is, when you're willing to live on the edge a bit and let your shit get brought up on a regular basis, it's amazing what wonderful things happen. **Instead of avoiding our shit, if we lean right into it (pardon the visual), it can be incredible.** Having my shit brought up gives me what I live for as a healer: opportunities for growth.

Susan suggested we check out a different beach. We jumped into the car and sped off. At another beach, we saw some nice waves, and though they were a bit too close to shore, they were surfable. I saw Susan relax a little – but only a little. We could work with the waves at the new beach, but they were still untested.

We slept peacefully that night. The next day, we went to the second beach with the retreat participants and the waves were huge compared to the day before! And the wind was howling. Man, THAT BROUGHT UP MY SHIT ... and Susan's, and – from the looks on their innocent faces – the retreat participants'. I stood and stared at the waves, wondering what to do. Then Susan made a decision.

In calm, lightly breezy conditions favorable to untested 45-year-olds, Susan was a fabulous surf instructor. But this was a whole different story. **The strong currents and powerful gusts had turned our sunny playground into a surf-pocalypse waiting to happen.** Susan's decision was to ask for help. She quickly found a wonderful surfing instructor who, with Susan's assistance, guided many of our participants to catch their first waves that very afternoon. It turned out to be nonapocalyptic and even quite awesome. Susan's shit had gotten brought up, but she'd found a resourceful way to get through it, which saved the day.

One of the retreat participants was also a brave warrior. We found out that in her early twenties, while swimming in the Pacific at night, she'd been held down – in surfer's lingo, **"caught inside"** – a pummeling set of large waves and had nearly drowned. Now in her 50s, she faced her shit on her own terms. She walked straight into the water. She said that finally returning to the ocean was like having "an incredible, soothing, liquid massage." She promptly began boogie boarding, lighting up the whole beach with her huge grin. **She stared down her shit, walked right into the monster's maw, and came out grinning.**

> ## Groundedness is next to Godliness.
> ## Engage your mind and truly
> ## challenge your body.
>
> " *Alice*

At dinner that night, we began to remember and recount experiences that BROUGHT UP OUR SHIT: feeling left out, being shushed, being bossed around, confronting the unknown, helicopter flights, sharks … **Life is packed with opportunities for having your shit brought up. It's what you do when your shit has been brought up that makes the difference.**

Often, we find our power by just diving into the thing that scares us. When we're willing to try, to take a step forward, to risk, we're often rewarded. In my experience, nothing is as terrible as our minds tell us it is. As Eleanor Roosevelt (one of the greatest FREAKS of all time) said, **"You must do the thing you think you cannot do."** If success follows, HUZZAH! If failure follows, you're one step closer to success.

As for me and my shit on that retreat, my preparations were fine and my fears of nonharmony proved to be unwarranted. The women on the retreat were some of the most amazing, courageous, open-hearted, and kind women I've ever traveled with. We got along like a house on fire.

———————————

✤✤ So, what BRINGS UP YOUR SHIT?

✤✤ How could you walk into that monster's maw?

✤✤ What kind of support can you ask for to help you go ahead with something that's important, even though it BRINGS UP YOUR SHIT?

Kicking it as hard as you do requires
deep, restorative sleep. If things are
difficult, get through whatever you must,
then get thy carcass to bed early.

" *Alice*

IS FOR

UPPER LIMIT

One of my absolute favorite questions to ask myself and others is **"How good are you willing to let it get?"** – because the only thing keeping us from what we desire is ourselves. If you were born to FREAK, you may want to read that again. Yes, you. I try not to spring that question on my clients until they already like and trust me, as it's a bit salty and to the point. But since I'm a life coach and not a life couch, **I will ask it.**

Whether knowingly or unknowingly, many of us have installed glass ceilings over our own lives. Gay Hendricks calls this our UPPER LIMIT. When I heard about this, I realized I was living under a glass ceiling of my own design, which precluded me from having the life I said I wanted. I could see what I wanted, but somehow couldn't get to it. The closer I got, the more frustrated I got.

Wherever our UPPER LIMIT is, that's how good we'll allow our life to get, overall. It can get *that good,* but that's it. To get to the *really* good stuff, to the place we *really* yearn to be, we must somehow raise that glass ceiling ... or dissolve it entirely.

Let me illustrate.

I'd been practicing pathology for about twelve years and, with the aid of life coaching, was loving life and feeling joyful at work every day. I'd gradually shifted into working part-time and so had more time to do other things I also loved. Life was great. **The universe had become a friendly place again.**

I began to feel pulled toward helping others find their own balance. I strategized about it and embarked on a sabbatical from work. One of the things I did during that time off was train as a coach. About halfway through my coach training with Martha Beck, I realized what I longed to do … and it wasn't surgical pathology.

I realized that I missed humans and I missed the freedom to be creative. I was stumped about how to proceed, so I asked the universe to help me figure out how to quit my job as a pathologist and pursue being a coach. I had a mortgage and four little honey badgers (see "R is for RECKLESS DISREGARD") to clothe and feed, so my income was needed.

A month later, **my husband was told that his monthly income would be increased by the exact amount of my paycheck. Really?** We rejoiced. I was so excited. I didn't have to go back to work after my sabbatical! I had choices!

Glee gave way to calm and then back to worry again. I began to entertain the thought that I couldn't quit my job, even though the issue of money had been solved. **Why wouldn't I say yes to what I'd said I wanted?**

It was because of that glass ceiling – my self-imposed UPPER LIMIT. I looked at the situation and realized I had beliefs that went something like this: "Life shouldn't be this easy" and "You have to work hard and sacrifice" and "You can't trust ease" and, worst of all, "You don't deserve to be this happy and worry-free about money." **Sheesh. Apparently, my left brain was having a heyday dreaming up reasons I couldn't have what I wanted.** When I realized that, I took a deep breath and said, "Yes, please" to my new choices.

To understand why we impose UPPER LIMITS on our lives, you could research the neuroscience, then you could do some cognitive behavioral therapy or neurolinguistically reprogram yourself, but (as always), I recommend the shortcut:

Ask yourself, "How good am I willing to let it get?"

 Where in your life have you already been given a green light from the universe, yet you continue to question whether it's okay to have what you desire?

 How good are you WILLING to let it get?

Allow Myself to Introduce Myself

PLUCKY
SURVIVOR

PLUCKY SURVIVOR

At the end of my sophomore year in college, I was diagnosed with malignant melanoma, which my boyfriend discovered. I didn't know what melanoma was. Turns out, it's a sometimes deadly type of skin cancer.

I had to have most of one entire buttock, all the way down to the muscle, removed by a kindly surgeon. I swear that **my buttock grew back in less than 24 hours (butts are strangely, and thankfully, resilient that way).** Post-surgery, I noticed that my parents had taken to spontaneously weeping around me. Finally, I asked what the deal was. They gently explained that they were sad because melanoma could kill me. **"WHAAAAAT??!!"** All of a sudden, my mortality hit me squarely in the face.

Facing my own mortality changed everything. I was in no way suicidal about it. Quite the opposite, in fact. **I began to take life a lot less seriously.** If I might die soon, then why not fucking enjoy the ride, right? I wanted to *live*. That fall, I did what I'd planned to do before my death threat: I flew to Scotland to live abroad for a year.

Of course, there was much seriousness involved with the melanoma, even though I was living abroad. I endured chest x-rays and lymph node exams. I traveled by train to the University in Edinburgh several times to undergo full-body skin exams, with a half-dozen medical students looking on. (Yikes! Being fully naked in front of a bunch of people of the opposite sex of approximately your own age is something I recommend only if you want to experience maximal humility.)

Between visits to doctors and studying physics and chemistry, I ran along the North Sea coast beaches while listening to the moody songs of Ten Thousand Maniacs. I drank, partied, clubbed, and danced endlessly to Rick Astley remixes while wearing all black. I ate kebabs with extra sauce at three a.m. I sang in Gilbert and Sullivan opera clubs. I dated several absolutely fascinating men. I went to Royal Air Force balls where they routinely force everyone present to drink seven or more shots (raising our glasses "To the Queen!"). **In short, I lived. I lived large.**

Oddly, having a brush with death made me aware of the part of me that wanted to *live*. By experiencing a *little death*, I **became reawakened to the life I was already and still living.**

In shamanism, an initiate is often killed or dismembered in their dreams or spirit journeys to give them an experience of death and merging with the cosmos. When I experienced this form of death, I learned how it feels to be an ecstatic part of the cosmos. This experience, just like my earlier brush with death, made me freer to live in this world in a more courageous way.

V IS FOR VIBRATION

Everything – yes, everything – has a VIBRATION, a spirit. In the shamanic world, we say, **"Everything that IS, is alive."** This includes books, peonies, stones, the ground you stand on, lip gloss, Italian tiles, and sweaters. A mentor once told me it took him five years of shamanic work before he truly downloaded this idea.

When we're getting ready to transform our lives in a major way, we often get strange urges to do things – like cut off all our hair, buy a new sofa, or purge our closets. That's **your soul, your inner genius, your heart, working to connect you to what's new that's growing inside you**, even if you can't yet verbally define it.

> Stop caring who's noticing, listening,
> or watching. Do it for you. Even if
> it means being a DAMN FOOL.
>
> " *Alice*

Those little urges are forming and hammering out the new you that's emerging. In such times, objects and outfits can speak to you VIBRATIONALLY, calling out your name. **I'm not talking about Imelda Marcos's compulsive shopping lust.** I'm talking about strange new whispers emanating from the new you that's being born.

I remember the day I received my very first Tracy Porter catalog. I stood dumbfounded in my foyer. I practically had to sit down and fan myself. That catalog absolutely riveted me. In it, gorgeous Tracy pranced around her rural farm in bohemian ensembles and settings that included crazy jewelry, chickens, and chandeliers. Her husband and four little kids joined in, frolicking in the delightful, gypsied interiors.

At the time, I was living in blue scrubs, Gap khakis, and Oxford shirts in a very formal home, and my children were in childcare much of the time. The images from that Tracy Porter catalog were about as far and away from my life as I could imagine. **Well,** I mused darkly, **there must be some sort of something wrong with that family. Could they really have lives of such pitch-perfect creativity and freedom, frolic and beauty?**

I was completely enchanted. **I proceeded to have a large shopping accident**, during which I bought nearly half the catalog's wares. Although I was miserable and exhausted most of the time from working nearly full-time and dealing with four kids, **on the bright side, I had some cash!** Sometimes, strangely, shopping in this way can bring you a clue to your happiness. (Notice I said "a clue," not "actual happiness.")

In one of the five boxes that arrived was a coat. When I first donned Brazilian designer Cecilia Prado's three-quarter-length sweater coat, with its gold threads and bohemian ethnic patterns, I thought **"Wow, could I actually wear this anywhere outside my closet?** What would people think?" I adored the coat, yet I felt a tad terrified. It was clearly a departure from my blue scrubs.

I decided to put safety first and experiment with wearing my wild new coat while on vacation with a friend in Manhattan. When I did, astonishing things happened! Several people stopped me on the street to tell me how beautiful the coat was. Typically jaded New Yorkers shopping at ABC Carpet and Home strained to get a glimpse of my new wonder coat. **Even heterosexual men clambered to quiz me about where I'd found it.** "Did you say Tracy Gorter?" "No," I patiently replied, "Tracy Porter, with a P. Do you want me to write it down for you?"

Wearing that coat marked the beginning of something magical. **The incredible beauty of that coat connected me to something beautiful inside myself that others could see.** I felt more alive in that coat than I had in a long time (and I still do feel alive when I wear it). It symbolized a more colorful, expressive, free life – a life that included children, chandeliers, chickens, and more joy.

> Declutter your lair. Your life.
> Let go of what doesn't work.
> Unleash the Feng Schwing.

Every single object in your home, every piece of clothing in your wardrobe, indeed everything, has its own VIBRATION and is alive. It can speak to you. When you're drawn to designs or styles that seem odd for you (or that might distress your mother), you may be onto something. You may be tuning in to the beginning of your newly magical life.

Noticing the VIBRATIONS of things is important for us FREAKS. Letting go of what doesn't feel good and welcoming what does helps us thrive.

 When you listen closely to the things currently in your life, what do they say to you? Do you hear "Bring me out and dust me off" or "Hurry up and pass me on to someone who needs me and will really love me," or something else altogether?

 What objects that you come into contact with as you go about your day seem especially to be saying "Pick me! Pick me!" to you?

Allow Myself to Introduce Myself

BEAN ARTIST

BEAN ARTIST

When my life had become terribly complicated, I was living in a six-thousand-square foot house and feeling overwhelmed and unhappy. I began getting strange urges. I'm not talking about sexual domination yearnings or cravings for Oreo cookies. These were Elmer's Glue–focused fantasies. I started doing decoupage.

For the uninitiated, decoupage is the delicate and often messy art of gluing paper onto stuff like glass or wood. I became obsessed with finding Victorian-ish images of bears and chickens and rabbits and other Beasties. This urge was so pronounced that my comedian sister, Maria, even told jokes about it: Sarah to Maria: **"DUDE! Grab a mug or a tray! What do you want to do? A rabbit or a moose? Let's decoupage!"**

If you'd seen me at night – exhausted, schlumped over the glowing computer screen, poring over the images I'd started collecting, scanning them from vintage postcards – you'd have thought I'd gone mad. My husband would say, "Aren't you ever coming to bed?" I'd say, "Yes … in just a few minutes," as I intently studied a newly discovered rabbit in a blue-striped suit.

As I decoupaged, I had no idea what the hell was happening to me or why I was so obsessed with all that imagery. I thought maybe I was supposed to be making stuff with the images I was drawn to, so I did: candles, trays, and flower holders, with lions, tigers, and oceans full of coral and fish. I even bravely went to the big city with a dear friend to schlep my creations to the shops. I sold some and even got some commissions (well, okay, one commission, from my mother's friend, for a golden retriever serving tray, which I never did complete).

Though I got some positive feedback, I was spending hours I *really* didn't have on decoupaging trays, which (by then) filled the entire dining room, and **I kept feeling like what I was doing wasn't exactly what I was supposed to be doing.** It was rawwwther frustrating. But I kept at it. I couldn't stop.

Share your dreams with visionary people,
with other FREAKS, who encourage you
and goad you into action.

" *Alice*

Then my friend Suzi joined me in my decoupage fantasy world. At night, we'd sit like complete loons in my basement decoupage laboratory making whimsical journals, decorating old green-bean cans (it really didn't matter much what we decorated), and singing along to awesome pop music. At 10:30, covered in glitter and glue, we'd line up our newest creations, look at each other, and I'd say, "But what does it *mean*??" I kept trying to understand why I was compelled to do what I was doing. **I wanted a logical reason for all my illogical activity.**

Suzi and I opened a tiny shop together, where we sold fixed-up vintage furnishings and some of our decoupaged creations. Our shop was about more than just selling things. It was as if we were both finding our own selves among the rubble of the garage sales and flea markets we'd troll through, seeking hidden treasures to resurrect with a little paint and placement into a vignette in our shop. What happened was that **by committing a bit of ourselves to our creativity, we rebirthed ourselves.**

Your process can be messy.
Allow yourself to work in a
way that works for you.

" *Alice*

The most freeing thing about that time – the decoupaging and the little shop – was allowing myself to do it purely for enjoyment. There was no need for any of it to make money (that was what my "real" job was for), or even to make sense. When I tried to make sense of it or figure out how I could make a living at it, I only became frustrated, but when I allowed myself to *just be an artist*, it all became utterly fantastic and joyful and I experienced what I now know is called *flow*.

I decided to post a sign in my creative lab in the basement that said **"JUST BE AN ARTIST"** – to remind myself that none of it had to make sense. I was beginning to claim the part of myself that's truly creative. Though I'd always loved to paint and draw and create in all mediums whenever I had the chance, over time and through schooling and exposure to the harsh and sometimes cruel world, at some point I'd come to believe that I wasn't an *artist* and that the title of artist was only for professionals.

I made my glittery "JUST BE AN ARTIST" sign myself. When I proudly showed it to my husband, he misread it. **"JUST BEAN ARTIST?"** he said, with a confused look. "Oh, so you're going to make stuff out of beans and pasta noodles? I did that in school. Yeah, I get it." **Dagnabbit!** Even making a sign about what I was going through didn't help the people close to me understand. It was maddening! Looking back, I see now that I was trying to convey a message to the world and to claim my own inner multitude, by saying, **"I AM AN ARTIST."**

After a while, I got tired of all the mess and the gluing, and it felt good to stop creating in that way. About a year later, while on sabbatical and spending a lot of time in the woods, I stumbled onto the idea that aligning ourselves with certain wild animals, or Beasties, is very powerful medicine indeed for whatever ails us. In that idea, in a way, **I rediscovered my life's purpose: to heal others using ancient, Earth-based methods.**

Perhaps the Beasties I spent so much time feverishly gluing onto glass during those few years knew all along that I truly am an artist, and they showed up to help me remember that.

It was necessary and healing to spend time in my quirky basement decoupage laboratory. In the process of allowing myself to simply create without rules, I began to understand that I could create *anything* my heart desires. **I learned that within me dwells a true artist.**

I still love to collaborate with others to design books, websites, and paper goods, and I still adore making things and combining different imagery elements, but I find it much less overwhelming now to work virtually through my computer.

Through it all, I've realized that I don't have to **try to** become an artist. I can just **BEAN ARTIST.**

sarah bamford seidelmann m.d. | www.borntoFREAK.com

W IS FOR

WHY AM I CONCERNED?

We who were born to FREAK are superlatively sensitive to the feeling states and vibes of others. We can't help it. FREAKS acutely sense others' feelings — elation, pain, celebratory joy, anger, agony, you name it — and **some of us merge with them into that feeling state.** This is known as empathy.

What a fabulous thing it is to join with someone in joy or enthusiasm or passion. It's scintillating and wondrous and amazeballs. But, for FREAKS, the downside of empathy is that if we merge into someone else's state of sadness, rage, or despair, we feel those feelings, too. We tend to do it out of love or because we care deeply, and then we want to fix it, solve it, make their pain go away.

So why is that bad? Shouldn't FREAKS want to help others? Sure, helping out is good and noble, but it's also a good idea to ask yourself why you're concerned.

"WHY AM I CONCERNED?"

This question can help you know whether you're relating to someone from a place of empathy or a place of compassion. **I've found that to really help others, it's best for FREAKS to resist the urge to merge in empathy** and to come instead from a place of compassion.

Compassion is being open-hearted enough to see, sense, or know that someone (another human, a Beastie, or any being) is troubled ... and yet not let that upset us or shift us out of balance in any way. We remain fully rooted in our own existence and our own feeling state. **It's like standing on terra firma and watching someone free-fall from a cliff high above ... and not panicking.** We know it's someone else, not us, who's falling from the sky. By not merging with what we sense to be their sheer terror and panic, we keep our wits about us so we can be present to witness whatever happens ... and, if necessary, to composedly call 911.

Empathy – that urge to merge – may be valuable as a way to understand others, but it's not particularly helpful if we want to aid someone who's in distress. When I empathize, if you're scared, I'm scared, too. That's how riots start. Individual fears are magnified as people merge with the feeling states of each other without keeping clear about whose feelings they're really feeling. People can become very distressed and anxious together very quickly. It's called emotional contagion, and it's powerful stuff.

The next time you're concerned or upset about someone who's suffering, check in with yourself and ask "WHY AM I CONCERNED?"

 Do you think you know what's best for them? (Do you really, actually know what's best for them?)

② Does their suffering make you feel sad or afraid, too? (Have you already started merging with their feelings? Yikes! Put on the brakes!)

③ Is any of this any of your beeswax?

④ Have you been asked to help?

I've learned that **the only life I can be an expert on is my own.** Everyone has been placed here to live out their own unique life (in the same way we FREAKS were born to FREAK). **When I want to help and think I know what's best for someone else, I know I'm in deep trouble.**

> **HELPING OTHERS** *Even when I'm dealing with my kids, I try to check in with myself and ask "WHY AM I CONCERNED?" Kids are often pretty damn wisdom-filled. I try to remember that as often as possible.*

For thousands of years, powerful shamanic healers (who, naturally, were born to FREAK) in tribal cultures knew they could only help if they were asked to help. Shamans didn't go around looking for troubled people to fix, heal, or help. Their healing work was only done with permission.

How the heck do I know what's right for someone else? Thinking I do is like saying to the other person, "I don't trust you to have the intelligence or wisdom to know what to do here, so I'll advise you, fix you, save you." If the person has hired you as a consultant on fashion, nutrition, skydiving, or whatever, and so has actually asked for your expertise, then, by all means, let them know about your recommendation to wear less velour, sprinkle kale dust on the steak tartare, or use a parachute. In all other cases, ask yourself, "WHY AM I CONCERNED?"

Is the trouble or upset you sense in another really your beeswax? Out of empathic concern, have you jumped in to help without being asked? I'm not talking about random acts of kindness, but random acts of advice-giving, repairing what's not yours to repair, and codependent meddling. Such merged urges may do more harm than good.

I find it useful to assume that *everyone* **is given the same access to divine guidance, higher power, the spirits, and "the way."** No one is truly alone. And sometimes, the only way someone can find their own way is to find it by themselves. Jumping in uninvited may not help that process.

Asking myself "WHY AM I CONCERNED?" is a daily practice for a FREAK like me. I'm not perfect, but **I work every day to stay in my own pasture and tend my own garden.** That helps me avoid jumping the fence and trampling all over someone else's project, or trying to water their patch with my hose from my side of the fence. Breathing helps, too.

Particularly with close friends and family – those we love dearly – empathy may be our default setting. We have so much love for them that standing in compassion without merging in empathy can be the toughest move in the business. In such cases, and if asked for help, we can invite them to visit their friendly neighborhood shaman, join a support group, or find a coach.

All of us FREAKS were born to inspire, heal, and change the world with our work – whatever that looks like and however we define it – through the photos we take, the poems we write, the earrings we mastermind, the food we cook, the deals we broker, the sandwiches we cut the crusts off of, the shows we produce, the songs we sing. At our very best, we create as compassionate beings. **By loving our own lives and our own** work, we inspire others to find their own best ways out of their pain.

Resisting the urge to merge with the dispirited emotional states of others and instead standing in compassion keeps us empowered in our own lives and affords us the composure to toss a parachute to someone who's free-falling ... if that's what they're asking for.

The next time you have the urge to merge with someone who's sad, dispirited, angry, or anxious, instead of joining them emotionally, consider how you could try stepping back a teeny bit, staying grounded in yourself, and offering support from that place?

When you're feeling low,
shut the front door. Try not to speak,
take big action, or make big decisions.
That will prevent many problems.

" Alice

X IS FOR

XANADU

The original XANADU was the glorious, lush summer capital of Kublai Khan, the emperor of China from 1260-1294. According to Marco Polo, a Venetian traveler who visited Kublai during his reign, XANADU was absolutely stunning, with a marble palace, huge gardens, meadows, rivers, game parks, and ferocious pet Beasties, including gyrfalcons and leopards. Some of the ultraluxe buildings were constructed of cane and silk cord and could be collapsed and transported in case Kublai decided to bust a move to somewhere else fabulous at the end of the summer.

Apparently, Samuel Taylor Coleridge was reading about XANADU when he fell into an opium-assisted dream that inspired the poem "Kubla Khan," which became one of the best-known poems in the English language. Thanks to Coleridge, XANADU became a symbol for splendidly luxurious and opulent places.

Back in XANADU's heyday as the summer palace, it apparently took three days on horseback to reach it. I'm thinking that by the time people arrived they were pretty stoked to discover the insanely elegant yurts with gilded interiors, dining rooms that could seat up to six thousand guests, and an emperor being carried around by his handlers on a jewel-encrusted throne while petting a leopard on a leash. **Sort of an ancient Chinese Graceland.** I imagine that arriving in XANADU would be like going glamping after running a marathon in a desert.

G*LAMPING is a glamorous alternative to traditional camping. It's practiced and touted by stylish, luxury-loving people who prefer less dirt and more comfort and chic in their camping experiences.*

I used to long for the kind of opulence and splendor found at XANADU – fancy marble palaces decorated with incredible gilding and painted by hand. I still do get contact highs when I flip through the latest issue of *Elle Decor*. Beauty and fabulous design soothe me, for sure. And yet ... after owning many things and having many experiences that might be considered luxurious (acid-washed marble kitchen countertops, crystal chandeliers, trips to African game reserves, body wraps), I have to say that **my favorite opulence is the kind that's intangible**, the kind that's free and not very hard to find, if you know where to look.

To rapidly terminate an emotional descent, DISENGAGE. Quick! Grab a fire extinguisher. Remember your FEEL GOOD, dammit, and get back to it.

" *Alice*

I often find my XANADU in the woods. My hunch is that Kublai Khan chose the site of his summer palace because of its natural opulence and splendor, its flowing rivers and amazing flowers and wild Beasties, for the natural expanse of it, and for the freedom and beauty it gifted to those who went there.

Nature is all of that and a bag of chips. FREAKS can benefit ginormously from a daily dose of beauty, of XANADU. When you spend time *out there*, immersed in nature, you can collapse its beauty, like one of Kublai's gilded yurts tied up with silk rope, and take XANADU with you, so you feel opulent and splendorous within, no matter where you are.

 In what places have you experienced true opulence and splendor, the kind that can only be sensed and accessed from within?

 What were the ingredients that made up that luxurious experience?

 How do you currently find your XANADU, or where might you look for it?

Y IS FOR

YOU

FREAKS need occasional (even frequent) relief from the hubbub of daily life. We FREAKS can find relief and inner peace in lots of ways that are easy, effective, and free. It's nice to keep it simple. Lately, I find that flinging myself onto the grass in the backyard works. Naps are nice. Hiking in the woods helps.

YOU often have more energy than the
average bear. Walk it off. Try parkour.
Do gymnastics. Run hard. Dance freely.
Allow YOUR energy to flow daily,
lest it emerge in awkward ways
with untoward effects.

I used to think that anyone normal who's exhausted and tired found relief at a spa. I originally got this idea from a dear friend with six kids who got weekly massages. She seemed to be the most serene and happy person I knew. I told myself I didn't have time for massages, as I was a full-time doctor, an übermother, a devoted wife, and all of that. But that was before enlightenment,

Grasshopper. (Okay, before partial enlightenment, as, Lord knows, I still have a long way to go.)

One midwinter day I somehow managed to get the day off from work when my children weren't sick. I put them in day care and decided that self-care was paramount (Gasp! What will the other übermothers think?). I deserved to feel good, I told myself. I needed relief. So **I made an appointment for a body wrap.** What could possibly go wrong?

A body wrap sounded more interesting than a massage and promised glowing skin to boot. While in medical school I'd had a massage, during which the massage artist (she was no Picasso) wouldn't stop talking and asking me medical questions. I'd walked away from that massage with two new problems: a stiff neck and fifty bucks less. I tried to block out that experience and dream of nirvana via body wrap. **A body wrap sounded life-changing. And it was.**

I sat in the waiting area at the salon, studying various birch-bark-infused wonder salsas I could apply to various parts of my body to quench or fan the flames of my internal fires. Abruptly, a rawwwther stern female attendant walked in and called my name. She took me to a changing room and brusquely instructed me to undress and put on a robe, saying she'd fetch me in a few minutes. I did as instructed, but when the attendant came back in a few minutes, it was to tell me I had a phone call on line one. Ruh roh.

It was the sitter. Apparently, **my six-year-old, who had a penchant for cleaning, had sprayed our pug, Buttercup, all over with window cleaner** in a valiant attempt to wash her. Good Gawwwd. Not sure how toxic the window cleaner might be to poor Buttercup, I called the vet. It was decided that rinsing

Buttercup thoroughly in the tub would be the best solution. Crisis averted. It was hard to escape the whacked-out madness of my life. But I was trying. I took a few deep breaths and resumed my wrap adventure.

The attendant took me to a room where there was a large coffin-like unit and instructed me to remove my robe and lie down in the coffin (she used some official term for it, but I've blocked it out). She didn't seem chatty, so I started to relax a bit and tried to go with the flow. She left the room while I disrobed – I assumed to grab some birch-paste salsa or whatever.

I lay there patiently, buck naked, in the coffin, which was hard and cold and gave me an unsettling foreshadowing of what it might feel like to lie in a real coffin. **When the attendant returned with a bowl of herbaceous paste, she seemed a tad alarmed by the sight of me, as though something was not quite right.** She sighed loudly, almost as if in defeat, and started coating me from stem to stern with some sort of Paste of Deep Peace and Relaxation, using what I can only describe as a spackling spatula.

After spackling me, the attendant massaged the paste into my skin with a gentle grinding motion, which made me feel much like I imagine a roast feels as it's being rubbed down with spices. She stopped a few times to assess the situation, perhaps to be sure she'd covered all the bases. **She gave another weird, subtle headshake of disbelief, then shut the lid of the coffin.** It was a coffin for the living, designed so my head could stick out – thankfully, because, as nutty-cakes as my life was, I wasn't considering checking out just yet.

When she cranked up the coffin roaster dial, my wrap experience kicked into high gear. Mmmm, I thought as I warmed up, maybe this isn't a coffin after all, but a Crock-Pot for the carcass. **I felt the way a tamale must feel as it steams inside its corn husk.** Warning me that it might get pretty hot and uncomfortable, the attendant told me that, to be on the safe side, she'd do a coffin-side vigil.

I'm not gonna lie. It was pretty weird to slow-roast in the buff in a coffin after being paste-rubbed by a gruff attendant. Still, it was definitely an improvement over that long-ago massage. I felt quite safe as I lay there just breathing, with my stern, silent, concerned attendant watching over me. It might even have been better than being at home. I drifted off a little.

When I awoke, I felt like I was dying of heat exhaustion. I violently pushed up the hinged lid of the coffin (resurrection!) and gasped for air. I was so hot!! The attendant (who, I suddenly noticed, bore a distinct resemblance to Nurse Ratched), chuckled and said in a low voice, unimpressed, "I told you it can get uncomfortable." **She got out a garden-hose-like contraption and began blasting the herbal paste off me,** keeping her distance, as if watering bee-infested honeysuckle bushes, or maybe more like hosing down car mats loaded with spilled ketchup. I sneaked a peek at her through one squinted eye and saw that she still looked somewhat bewildered.

Yes, in the end, my skin was softer, but the whole experience had left me feeling oddly unsettled. The next week, I got my hair cut at the same salon and the stylist asked how my wrap had been. To be completely frank, I told her, it had felt really odd to be **buck naked in a coffin and rubbed like a roast,** but, I concluded, it wasn't half bad. The stylist started laughing then. She laughed uncontrollably, so hard she gasped for air and had to hold onto the salon chair for support. Finally, she was able to get out the words, **"Didn't they tell you to wear a bathing suit?"** No, good madam, they did not.

Suddenly, it all became clear. My stern spa attendant's concerned and bewildered looks came from her buttoned-up spa sensibilities, which were offended by my protocol-free "all Sarah all the time" centerfold show. Sigh. Yes, I was born to FREAK, but a spa was certainly not the place to do it. Listen, people, if YOU can't let YOUR hair down (or YOUR towel) and get fully naked at the spa, where can YOU?

Get a daily dose of PHYSICAL PLEASURE.
Laughter. Hugs. Great sex. Massage.
Kisses. Tickles. Soft sweaters.

Discover what feels GOOD
and prioritize it!

" *Alice*

There are so many faster, cheaper, more fun, less hot, less naked, and less horrifying ways to take time for YOU and find relief as a FREAK than subjecting YOURSELF to a naked body wrap. **I suffered in the coffin, but YOU don't have to.**

I invite YOU to find simple ways to spell relief for YOU. Take a nap. Disappear from view for fifteen minutes. Go for a walk in nature. Call a friend.

 How can YOU find relief without it being overly complicated, expensive, or involving roasting in a coffin (unless YOU really enjoy that)?

Alice's Call to Slackers

"They say the wisest of all animals, the most

powerful and divine of all beings, is the elephant ...

and really the look of wisdom in a big elephant

is tremendously impressive."

– Carl Jung

*(Alice the Elephant feels that the topic of non-doing is so **extra-important** it deserves its own chapter, which she **insisted** on writing.)*

Hello, humans. It is me, Alice the Elephant and Life Obstacle Assassin. I'm writing this chapter because I want you to remember one little thing: **Often, it is in the slacking that one achieves great things.** I don't care what anyone else says – please take your slacking seriously. The best slacker out there is the one having the most fun. I am *not kidding*.

slack
not tight or held tightly in position;
loose, like a goose

It's weird to elephants that humans lose their slacker focus and think they're *supposed* to be doing something *all the time*. Often, however, you are not. **Much of the time, in fact, you are supposed to be slacking.** So quit being such a *Wiener Schnitzel* about it and slack already!

Every one of the greatest humans in the universe became great *not* because of hard work, not primarily because of a brutalizing test or challenge they had to get through (yes, you will have those, too), but simply because they understood how to slack, so they did slack, and then they slacked some more, and they kept slacking until, one day, they woke up as (**SHAZAM!!**) master slackers!

> After intense bouts of creation,
> make like a slug.
>
> " *Alice*

It could happen to you. **We were all born for greatness.** As famous slacker Marianne Williamson wrote, "Our deepest fear is not that we are inadequate. Our deepest fear is that we are powerful beyond measure."

Sure, there may be dark days ahead. **Others may snort, scoff, or sneer as you lay idly on your inflatable dolphin on the lawn.** It's not easy to tell a bunch of people all hepped up on Diet Coke and fear that you won't be working extra hours this week because you'd rather slack for a few days.

Do it for you. **Through your slacking, others may be inspired to do the same.** Free yourself, so that others may also slack. (Also, do it because your mother wouldn't like it – at all.) Become the hero by connecting deeply to the slacker that lives within you.

I once observed Sarah slacking so hard in her home that she'd become sandwiched between two couch cushions, in what you might call a *couch canyon*. It felt very, very good. Then her kids started shouting at her – something about wanting a snack (for the third time in an hour), telling her she needed to quit slacking because they needed her ASAP!

In that moment, I watched Sarah reach down, down to a place deep inside and connected with her inner slacker, the one who knows no limits, the one who's connected to The Knower of All, and tell her children, quietly yet firmly, "No thank you. I'm going to keep slacking here for fifteen more minutes."

Sarah did it. You can, too. Human, it's imperative that you find your inner slacker!

Your inner slacker is ...

... the one who has you saying, "By *GAWWWD*, *nobody* will stop me from slacking! It's who I am. It's how I roll. Slacking is me. We are one. Slacking is most important. *You*, on the other hand, can wait."

... the one who can lay motionless for hours watching reruns of *Glee*, nourished only by a bag of microwaved popcorn and a bottle of kombucha with chia seeds.

... the one who *will not* get out of bed, because they know there's a better way and that better way does not, *under any circumstances*, involve getting out of bed.

... the one who spontaneously falls onto the grass and lies there staring at cloud formations, endlessly entertained by the s-l-o-w m-o-t-i-o-n show.

... the one who really doesn't give a damn if there are dust tumbleweeds a-tumblin' across the foyer.

... the one who spends a long time just looking at pretty pictures in books, having no use for words or the gaining of knowledge.

... the one who knows that exercise can also be a *mental state*, one that doesn't necessarily require breaking a sweat.

... the one who can shapeshift into a pug at will, snoring like nobody's beeswax in a coma-like state for hours.

My dear human friends, it's time to take slacking to a whole new level. I don't want to scare you, but this is, in fact, a new age. **In the age of abundance, if you can't slack, then you may well become a dinosaur!**

As a FREAK, you're being called to set an example of what it means to truly *slack*. To slack for real. Not half-assed slacking, but whole-assed slacking! You must slack with fully conscious intention. You must commit wholeheartedly to slacking. Go completely boneless and slack far beyond the cellular level. **The kind of slacking I speak of takes place on an ATOMIC level.**

Don't let anybody *ever* tell you that you can't slack. If they do, send them to me. Tell them there's one *large* and *salty* elephant named Alice who's kicking ass and taking names.

People! This is a revolution!

Take time daily to be all you cannot be!

Alice
The Elephant and Life Obstacle Assassin

   sarah bamford seidelmann m.d. | www.borntoFREAK.com

 IS FOR

ZUGUNRUHE

Over the past few years, I've spent a preposterous amount of time studying wild animal behavior as it relates metaphorically and literally to human behavior. As an animal totemologist who goes about her job vigorously, I've spent many marvelous hours in the pursuit of Beastie info – **bumping around** on the South African Bushveld in a Land Rover; **communing** with an eccentric and controversial animal rescuer while he wrestled and mothered orphaned bear cubs in West Virginia; **schmoozing** with Bob, the peregrine falcon guy, at Morro Bay; **birding** in Minnesota's Sax Zim Bog (a Dr. Seussian name for North America's premier winter birding destination); **banding, snuggling, and releasing** saw-whet owls under cover of night; **leading** recovering wild mustangs around in a pen; **tromping** with binoculars along the beaches of Lake Superior with world-renowned ornithologists wearing vests packed with birding tackle; **intensely bonding** with a nature photographer who, like me, could spend hours alone in the woods.

The most interesting things I discover about wild Beasties often have a deep resonance for me as a human.

On a lucky day in Sax Zim Bog with Erik Bruhnke – one of the finest guides of the avian world – **I learned the magical word ZUGUNRUHE** (say "ZOOG-oon-ROOha," with enthusiasm!). *ZUGUNRUHE* describes a peculiar behavior some Beasties exhibit when it's time to migrate or move on.

The German word **ZUGUNRUHE** comes from **ZUG** (move, migration) and **UNRUHE** (anxiety, restlessness). Birds in ZUGUNRUHE **appear to have their little birdy undies in tiny birdie bundles.** They're rawwwther anxious and fluttery and restless as hell. Basically, their birdie bodies are telling them in various ways that the time has come to go.

So, **what, pray tell, does ZUGUNRUHE have to do with humans?** We who were born to FREAK experience seasons in our lives, too. We FREAKS sometimes get an anxious or restless feeling, a ZUGUNRUHE telling us it's time to move on, literally or metaphorically, to something new. Maybe it's time for a new career or a new way of being in the world, a new project, a different kind of relationship.

Being in ZUGUNRUHE can be kind of disturbing, altering our sleep patterns, waking us up at night as we begin to realize that something's not right. **It can feel like it's no longer peaceful to stand still in this place.** Little yearnings start showing up as our undies begin gathering themselves into bundles. Those strange urges clue us in to where to fly to next, how we might get there, and when it's time to go.

As humans, we can sometimes forget (I forgot) that our bodies – just like birds' bodies – are hardwired to navigate for us. But if we tune in, we hear whispers. We may not be like the blackpoll warbler, which suddenly knows it's time to fly nonstop from New England to New Zealand ... but, then again, we might!

sarah bamford seidelmann m.d. | www.borntoFREAK.com

Human ZUGUNRUHE seems to express itself in many different ways. It can start with a discomfort that begins to rise, **an urge telling you that, like the birds, you just gotta fly ...** or be doomed to a lifetime of nervousness and chronic sleep disruption.

There are other symptoms of ZUGUNRUHE, too. I've experienced various periods of ZUGUNRUHE in my life, during which I've been wide awake at three a.m. for nights in a row and gained weight **(sudden mass gain, or polymorphism, is common in migratory birds during ZUGUNRUHE)**. Hell, once I even molted like a European robin, during a particularly intense ZUGUNRUHE-prompted episode of telogen effluvium – a human scalp condition that causes the simultaneous shedding of all hair in a certain growth stage (I had to vacuum a lot during that one).

For humans and Beasties, the keys to making a successful migration through a really big change are the same. Here are a few helpful tips:

 Know where you are. Assess your current literal and metaphorical location.

2 **Know the direction of your destination or goal.** What are you moving toward? Joy? Inner peace? Outer Mongolia? Get clear on what your destination looks, feels, tastes, and smells like.

3 **Maintain a course in that direction.** Check in during your journey, from beginning to end. Are you getting closer to your destination? If not, which wing flap needs to be adjusted?

 Know when to stop. Have you arrived yet? Look around.

If yes, then settle in. Build a nest or do whatever you need to do to get comfy ... until ZUGUNRUHE strikes again.

If you're experiencing ZUGUNRUHE, don't let your or anyone else's previous failed attempts to change keep you from honoring the whispers and shouts for something new.

Remember that you truly
cannot make a wrong turn.
So keep REACHING, DREAMING,
and ACTING on joyful impulses.

If you're experiencing a severe ZUGUNRUHE but feel unable to flap off toward the new place (physical or metaphorical), a wonderful coach or healer of some ilk (shamanic or otherwise) may be able to help you alleviate your discomfort and rediscover your own internal compass so you can use it to get to your lovely new destination. Then you can focus on settling in and enjoying your new bounty.

 Are you experiencing ZUGUNRUHE right now? What does that anxious, restless feeling seem to be whispering about a new destination?

 Are you molting? What's being shed? What new feathers are trying to come in?

Allow Myself to Introduce Myself

BUSHWHACKING ANTHROPOLOGIST

BUSHWHACKING ANTHROPOLOGIST

*"Anthropology is the science which tells us
that people are the same the whole world over,
except when they are different."*

– Nancy Banks-Smith

As my mother foretold ("I just know I'm going to want to sleep through those years"), my teen years were rough. My born-to-FREAK intensity, curiosity, and energy brought with them a desire to grow up quickly. FREAKS, like anthropologists, are especially talented at making observations, but if not careful, while on assignment in the bush, we can lose ourselves out there.

I've always been an intense observer of others. I remember standing miserably in the seventh-grade locker room, my eyes darting around to glance at the other girls as we donned our hideous, ancient, black, itchy regulation bathing garments. All the other bodies seemed to be developing nicely, but my body was definitely strange. **Odd tubular structures burst forth on my chest (ack! problem!)**. I certainly didn't feel like an exalted, celebrated, lithe *Seventeen* magazine–model version of normal. Instead, I felt very uncomfortable being abby-normal.

Prone to bouts of curiosity about the adult world and never one to tolerate being bored, I dove into trying many things. In one such episode, a friend and I dedicated ourselves to stealing nips of booze from different bottles so our explorations would go undetected. We then brilliantly combined them all in a Seven Seas salad dressing bottle, for elegant decanting. We swilled our concoction just before heading into school one morning in seventh grade. The results were less than positive.

sarah bamford seidelmann m.d. | www.borntoFREAK.com

All I remember is a camera flash bulb going off in homeroom and then running for the bathroom. As I puked into the toilet, Betty, the on-duty "buster" (as we fondly called the hall monitors), asked me what was wrong. In my drunken stupor, I stared at the graffiti-covered stall wall until I had the brilliant idea of saying, "I had chicken for breakfast, Betty, and it just didn't sit well." Miraculously, she believed me. She gently suggested I go ahead and walk home, which I did. I metabolized the Seven Seas cocktail much more comfortably at home, watching *The Price is Right* in my pink-gingham-wallpapered bedroom. My mother had no clue. I remember thinking it curious how little the adults in my life noticed what I was up to.

By the end of eighth grade, I was even more miserable. My terrified but emotionally intelligent parents noticed my misery and asked me if I wanted to transfer to a different school. I did, and it helped. I transferred to a mostly Catholic high school, even though my family wasn't Catholic (I'd been raised as a free spirit by my bohemian and Episcopalian parents).

Going to Catholic school was like getting a whole new lease on life, like going on assignment for *National Geographic* to study the inhabitants of a foreign land where the natives wore plaid skirts. My bushwhacking anthropologist self was in heaven.

Upon entering my new school, I took on a new role – that of a well-behaved *Seventeen* magazine-esque girl who wore clean-cut Lands End outfits. I swore off the Seven Seas and started anew, playing the role of a string-of-pearls-wearing, fine, upstanding citizen. Though my bush helmet was invisible, I was definitely there to observe and learn.

In Catholic school, I felt like I was being indoctrinated into a secret society, though it was one I could never actually belong to. My classmates fascinated me. Their life experiences, compared to mine, were quite odd. Almost everyone I polled had been instructed in the same ritualistic teachings. For example, their parents had told them, **"If you get pregnant, so help us God, we'll kick you out."** Wow! Strange! I asked them if they believed such teachings. "Sure," they replied without pause.

My mother, on the other hand, had told me that if I ever got pregnant, she and my father would take me to Planned Parenthood and help me figure out where to place the baby for adoption. They told me they'd support me all the way, without saying they'd raise the kid.

In the Catholic schools my fellow students had all attended from preschool on, the nuns were feared and revered and could be quite formidable. **According to reports shared by the natives, the nuns concealed knives in their leather boots and the hems of their habit skirts.** I'd never known such formidable people. Well, let me rephrase that. Before going to Catholic school, I'd seen nuns as holy and benevolent, but I hadn't seen the kind of respect and fear they seemed to inspire.

As I got to know the people in my new school, **I discovered that Catholics actually aren't all that different from the rest of us** (except maybe for the getting-kicked-out-of-the-house-if-you're-pregnant rule). We were actually more alike than we were different. They also listened to Madonna and liked to try on lip gloss and cruise around drinking 7-Eleven Slurpees. I had a motley posse of friends who helped me get through those years and by tenth grade we were all in cahoots together – finding ways to buy alcohol, smoke pot, and generally escape our pain.

With all the activities I did in high school and all the friends I had, you might have thought I was having a ball. And, I suppose, when I sang "I wear my sunglasses at night" at the top of my lungs while getting stoned with a friend, I thought I was. But **mostly high school felt defeating. It wasn't an easy place to embrace individuality and inner multitudes.**

Even back then, I was drawn to the artists and eccentrics. They were the ones who kept to themselves and, in secret, wrote a brilliant and EPIC work of satire lampooning our entire class. They showed up on Halloween courageously dressed as someone of the opposite gender. They hid the word *FUCK* in the year book's cover art. They were less afraid to FREAK than the rest of us. I felt a kinship with them, but found it hard to cross the lines drawn in high-school society, which made my interactions with them rocky, at best.

Since Catholic school, I've gone on many other anthropologic expeditions and learned how to more successfully cross boundaries. My anthropology explorations have included attending Hebrew Camp for three weeks (thanks to a Jewish friend I had in eighth grade, I ended up speaking better Hebrew than most Episcopalians I knew), being a foreign exchange student in the Dominican Republic, going to university in Scotland for a year, serving on a few medical missions to rural Honduras, living in Colombia for several months while adopting two of my children, and taking on a support role in a Lobola (bride price negotiation) in South Africa.

I've always found other people, cultures, religions, and ways of being in the world endlessly fascinating. The more I explore, observe, and learn, the more I love humanity. We truly are all more alike than we are different. **So many of us want the same things, despite our differences** in politics, religion, teenage pregnancy teachings, and breast shape. The amazing humans I've met on my adventures seem to simply want to feel good, to love and be loved, and to be accepted for who they are. Just like me.

I find it helpful to also apply my anthropological inclinations to myself, to return to myself and celebrate my own ways, my inner culture, and who I am at my core.

UNCOVER YOUR OWN MULTITUDES

A GUIDE

I thought it might be nice to give you a few ideas here about how you can uncover your own multitudes, in case reading about my strange multitudes has gotten you wondering about your own. (I hope it did!) Getting to know thyself is very, very good stuff, and loving thyself (and all your multitudes, once you find them) is highly recommended.

Sometimes when I'm dealing with a difficult question – like, **How can I explain to my dear readers how to discover their own inner multitudes?** – I ask Alice the Elephant for help, as she often has wise advice.

What Alice recommends is that you dive down into the ocean and look for a single perfect lotus there at the very bottom of the sea. Alice explained to me that this lotus represents you and that each petal is a facet of your wonderful and fantastic self.

I didn't get it. "But, Alice," I asked, "how do my readers figure out which petal represents what?" She chortled and suggested that you could **be still, meditate on your multitudes, or ask for a dream to show you one of your multitudes.** Well, they are directions, but they're not very detailed (Alice can be a little mischievous that way). Then our time together ended and Alice had to run off to take care of some elephantine business.

I think what Alice was trying to get at with her funky oceanic metaphors is that **you and your inner multitudes are as beautiful as a lotus.** Deep down within yourself, if you go diving for it, you can find the beauty of your multitudes. Petal by petal, you can discover the majesty of your born-to-FREAK self.

> Sit on a lotus already.
> Just be. Five minutes a day, minimum.
> Watch inspiration flow.

Since I was still not fully satisfied that I had what I need to help you, dear readers, I went back to Alice again the next day. I asked her, "Isn't there a simpler way to help, like with a pachydermally inspired worksheet, a shortcut, or something like that?" "No, "Alice said, "to find your inner multitudes you really must go to the source and look deep within. "Alice repeated her recommendations of sitting alone quietly, meditating, or going on a vision quest of some kind. She said that spending time alone with yourself is the key.

Because we are humans and not pachyderms, we often like worksheets and prompts and templates. I suggest using the blank worksheet below, filling it in for each petal of your multitudinous self. I've included an example, using one of my lotus petals. You'll also find a blank form for recording your inner multitudes, if that feels good to you.

See all the individual stars in your mind's sky. Soften your gaze and allow a new constellation to come into focus.

" Alice

Really, this is *your* life, and nobody but you can do your deep oceanic lotus diving. You alone are qualified. I'm terribly excited for you to discover your multitudes and celebrate them and bring them out to parade around for all to see, because when you do, the world will suddenly have become more beautiful. **I want to look up one day and see the world as a field of lotuses. Won't that be stunning?**

Now, off with you! Dive and seek your petals. And don't forget to come up for air every once in a while.

MY BEAUTIFUL
LOTUS SELF

I call this petal (multitude) ...

Mama-san or Mother/Night Club Manager.

This petal represents ...

my desire to mother all living things, including myself, and to throw fun parties so we can all connect and share the love.

I might have needed to have this sad or distressing experience so that I would recognize this beautiful inner petal:

Going to work every day and missing my children terribly.

I can (or could or did) safely begin to express this petal more fully by ...

paying attention and beginning to figure out how to work less and, eventually, how to work from home. Also, I kept throwing parties, even when it made no logical sense.

I currently use this beautiful petal ...

with my children, other people's children, my dogs, other animals, and whenever I'm at a party or throwing a party of any kind.

What I really dream of doing with this petal is ...

throwing a week-long party in Bali with my loved ones and other amazing born-to-FREAK people, where we volunteer at an elephant sanctuary, celebrate ourselves, and encourage ourselves to dream new dreams.

MY BEAUTIFUL
LOTUS SELF

I call this petal (multitude) …

_____

_____

_____

This petal represents …

_____

_____

_____

**I might have needed to have this sad or distressing experience
so that I would recognize this beautiful inner petal:**

_____

_____

_____

**I can (or could or did) safely begin to express this petal more
fully by …**

_____

_____

_____

I currently use this beautiful petal ...

_____

_____

_____

What I really dream of doing with this petal is ...

_____

_____

_____

My beautiful petals (multitudes) include these:

Petal

_____

Petal

_____

Petal

_____

Petal

_____

Petal

_____

sarah bamford seidelmann m.d. | www.borntoFREAK.com

Petal

Petal

Petal

Petal

Petal

(Use as many or as few lines as you need.)

Never apologize for your FREAKINESS.
It's not a defect to be surgically excised.
Good Gawwwd, it's a gift to be nurtured!

" *Alice*

sarah bamford seidelmann m.d. | www.borntoFREAK.com

BORN-TO-FREAK

HEROES

It can be so very helpful to find other born-to-FREAK people that you admire. Why? Well, it's said that we recognize qualities we admire because we possess those very same qualities.

I invite you to select three FREAKS to admire (below is a list of a few of my favorites, in case you'd like some inspiration). Once you've chosen your three, write down a few wild and woolly adjectives to describe their essence. For example:

Rachel Zoe: Irreverent and passionate.
Gandhi: Kind and resolute.
Ellen DeGeneres: Kooky and ridiculous.

Look at those wonderful adjectives ... and realize that those are qualities that inform your own multitudes. Ask yourself, **How could I be and/or do more of that in my own life? What would feel good? What would shift?**

You could create a mini-collage of your favorite born-to-FREAK heroes and put it up in your medicine cabinet, to peek at every time you brush your teeth. It takes courage to FREAK – we need great examples of what that looks like to inspire us daily.

MAXIMIZE time spent with humans and Beasties who get you and who love you. MINIMIZE contact with those who don't.

" *Alice*

My favorite FREAKS of fame and note are presented here for your admiration and inspiration.

Fashion FREAKS

Mary-Kate Olsen
Bill Cunningham
Simon Doonan
Grace Coddington
Tim Gunn
Rachel Zoe
Iris Apfel – style icon
The women of Ari Seth Cohen's Advanced Style blog

World-Changing FREAKS

Mahatma Gandhi
Mother Teresa
Ellen DeGeneres
Steve Jobs
Oprah
Mark Zuckerberg
Albert Einstein
The Dalai Lama
Patch Adams

Divine FREAKS

Teresa of Ávila
St. Augustine
Jesus
Alice the Elephant
Buddha
Ganesha
St. Francis of Assisi

Lao Tzu
Lakshmi

Surfing FREAKS

Jaimal Yogis, author of *Saltwater Buddha*
Dave Rastovich
Bethany Hamilton
Bill Hamilton and Sava (RIP) Surfing Dog
Laird Hamilton
Gerry Lopez

Poet FREAKS

Emily Dickinson
Sheila Packa
Maya Angelou
Robert Bly
Mary Oliver
Antonio Machado
Rumi
Hāfez
Dr. Seuss

Entertainment FREAKS

Ellen DeGeneres
Rainn Wilson
Ty Pennington
Jack Black
Jim Carey
Zooey Deschanel
Tina Fey
Alec Baldwin
Carson Kressley

Kristen Wiig
Stephen Colbert
Johnny Depp
Maya Rudolph
Betty White
Maria Bamford
Nora Ephron
Katherine Zeta-Jones
Brooke Shields
Emma Thompson

Filmmaker FREAKS

Steven Spielberg
Danny Boyle
Jud Apatow
Ang Lee

Fiction Writer FREAKS

Roald Dahl
Ernest Hemingway
Dr. Seuss
E.B. White
Lewis Carroll
Gertrude Stein
Anne Lamott
William Steig

Mainline music, dance,
nature, and community.

" *Alice*

sarah bamford seidelmann m.d. | www.borntoFREAK.com

Musical FREAKS

Kate Bush
David Bowie
Adam Levine of Maroon 5
Annie Lennox
Freddie Mercury
Elton John
Madonna
Adam Young of Owl City
Jason Mraz
Justin Timberlake

Science FREAKS

Linus Pauling
David Hawkins
Sylvia Earle
Jane Goodall
Albert Einstein
Stephen Hawking

Food FREAKS

Alice Waters
Kris Carr
Julia Child
Jamie Oliver

Famously Open ADD FREAKS

Edward Hallowell
Mary-Kate Olsen
Adam Levine of Maroon 5
Justin Timberlake

Beyoncé's younger sister, Solange Ty Pennington
Will Smith
Jamie Oliver
Michael Phelps

Self-Help Writer FREAKS

Deepak Chopra
Jaimal Yogis
Martha Beck
Marianne Williamson
Gay Hendricks
Mike Dooley
Andy Dooley
Jeannette Maw
Wayne Dyer
Shakti Gawain
Barbara Sher
Julia Cameron

Business FREAKS

Daniel Pink
Danielle LaPorte
Guy Kawasaki
Steve Jobs
Alicia Rittenhouse
Richard Branson
Tim Ferriss

Shamanic FREAKS

Clarissa Pinkola Estes
Mabel McKay
Michael Harner

Sandra Ingerman
Jeremy Narby
Alberto Villoldo
Robert Moss
Malidoma Somé
Colleen Deatsman
Timothy Cope

Beautiful-Product-Creating FREAKS

John Derian
Tracy Porter
India Hicks
Mincing Mockingbird
Frantic Meerkat
Jonathan Adler
Shy Nimitta
Kenspeckle Letterpress

Interior Design FREAKS

Kelly Wearstler
Kathy Ireland
Nate Berkus
Tony Duquette
Suzi Vandersteen
Kelly Hoppen
Nancy Lancaster
Mario Buatta
Bunny Williams

Imaginary FREAKS

Willy Wonka
The Lorax
Yoda
Tigger
Pooh
Alice in Wonderland

SuperFREAKS*

Steve Martin	fiction writer, banjo player, thespian, and comedian
Lady Gaga	multiple instrument wielder, designer, launcher, and lady of good works
Gwyneth Paltrow	cookbook writer, actress, singer, traveler

* FREAKS who freak in so many amazing directions they can't be categorized

THANKS ... SERIOUSLY

Dear Reader,

It is my greatest wish that this book somehow soothes and brings cheer and encouragement to those who, like me, were born to FREAK. There are so many of us quietly (or not so quietly) waiting for something to happen, for someone to tell us what we're meant to do, or for someone to approve of what we want to do. **I've discovered that life works best when we decide for ourselves what we want to do and go do it**, in whatever way possible. If you do that, you can't make a wrong turn. Your first inspired action will attract wonderful things, people, and experiences that delight you and help you do more of what you want to do.

That's how this book came together.

It's impossible for a FREAK like me to even think of writing a book without the league of amazingness that surrounds me.

Let me begin with *Grace Kerina*, my editor and shepherd, whose kindness, perfectly timed saltiness, and gentle herding techniques helped turn all my wild and bohemian musings into what I daresay is a rawwwther cohesive, cogent, and coherent volume. **I feel like I win the lottery every day I get to work with her.** There's nothing more exciting than waking up to an inbox of her notes because she's been busy in Germany caring for my words and ideas. Most of all, her questions taught me to probe deeper into myself and to love myself on a deeper level.

Connect with other wacky kooks and
FREAKS who goad you to more goodness.
Watch them SHINE. Glow along with them.

"*Alice*

Then there are all the FREAKS I've stumbled into in ordinary reality, who've shown me by their example what FREAKING looks like – by living fearlessly and authentically on a daily basis. I must thank these very special humans because **without their fearlessness, I'm not sure this book would've been written at all.** These FREAKS are (in no particular order) ...

Lisa Odenweller, for realizing that food is what excited her most, and for creating Beaming and B Bar.

Susan Honnell, for shining constantly, noticing all amazing dogs, and dancing while she packs her suitcase.

Amy Pearson, for being a brazen ladycat, donning hammer pants, dancing, and sharing it with all of us.

Donna Kramer, for her airport ambush story and for swimming in the ocean.

Martha Atkins, for just plain being fucking amazing, period, and for artful exercises and doing group healing sessions on behalf of others.

Joel Bamford, for throwing ginger snaps in the Chinaman Geyser, wearing huaraches, and doing things with a reckless disregard. *Rose Regier*, for Lady Gaga costumes and for her dream of traveling the world to record the stories of the tribe (I hope you do it!)

Indrani Goradia, for the Ass-Kicking Ceremony and for life-altering yoga and dancing ("If I was you, gurrrl ...")

Jaimal Yogis, for stealing money for a ticket to Hawaii and for opening his heart for all to see in his book *Saltwater Buddha*.

Ali Duffey, for her Mardi Gras gear, flashing green dragons, and eye for beauty.

Michael Pechinski, for reviving Polynesian dance and for the beautiful patterned fabrics he creates.

David Olson, for daily inspiration, for sharing Gladys (his pug) and tales from the hood, and for making the world smaller and more cozy.

Fabeku Fatunmise, for awesomesizing and for inviting others to reach for their own magic selves.

Jessey Gilbertson, for taking risks, donning feathered head-dresses, and being himself, unapologetically and beautifully.

Michael Harner, for eating coffee-flavored ice cream and making comedic comparisons between the underworld and New Jersey as he lives his mission.

Tamara Schafhauser, for doing the Dracula project and for doing work she loves every day.

Lisa Revoir, for daring to be happy, making amazing chocolate cake, being an amazing mom, and surfing the waves.
Krista Warren, for rooftop dancing and for being the most fun lady pathologist ever.

Krisa Christian, for wearing that blue tube top pantsuit that rocked and for fitting in fun in all the ways she does.

Janelle Holden, for tales of whiskey and fudge and making me laugh about things I hadn't even known were funny.

Marta Watson, for being unabashedly and awesomely herself and a champion of all Beasties.

Teresa Aldach, for DJ-ing with her sultry voice and for loving the music she loves.

Anna Kunnecke, for being a fearless speaker, human, and mama-san.

Sonja Vogen Baertsch, for free-falling with such grace and humility, and for saying, "Shoooot!"

Magdalena Solveig Walhoff, for *showing up* on Amberwing's committee and for leading companies that produce products that care for those who create them.

Susan Hyatt, for being a wolf momma for so many humans – teaching by example what's possible when we become warriors.

Barbara Swift, for her beautiful soul and for creating despacho ceremonies with things that are not from Michael's crafts stores.

Mary Beth Leisen, for being an exuberant and salty pilgrim on this road of life (please pass the shaman sauce).

Meghan Fordice, for being a most amazing mother to my children when I can't be there; and for being a beautiful, brave, and treasured friend.

 sarah bamford seidelmann m.d. | www.borntoFREAK.com

Alicia Gates, for her fierce and powerful teachings (I am sitting at your feet, listening and taking notes).

John Derian, for sticking to what "finally worked" and patiently creating his business, which is a gift to all who enter (his soul must be as stunning as his store is).

Tami McCall, for posing on the beach and letting us share that moment.

Susan Bainter Baghdadi, for acroyoga and taking others on pilgrimages.

Margaret Webb, for sharing her infectious joy, curiosity, and wisdom about nature and for being an amazeballs momma.

John Serpa, for finding ways to incorporate techno music and for being a storm-chasing enthusiast.

Mark Clark, for being so full of hope and enthusiasm, and for being a lover of life.

Kari Hazzard, for being unafraid, period.

Marc Berg, for being an MD who's tuned in to the natural universe (the only kind there is).

Janet Jones, for Russian animation, being beautiful, and seeing the comedy in self-help.

Natalie Bachir, for finding ways to incorporate her multitudes soooo beautifully.

Max Daniels, for being a curator of beautiful thoughts, like "Keep calm and ask for more."

Eleni Johnson, for cultivating her pure raw power (It's beautiful to see you express it!).

Kimberly Dawn, for being highly sensitive and highly awesome and creating the group that helped me understand a few things about being born to FREAK.

Maggie Thickens, for being an example of how *boardroom* = dance party, and for saying things under her breath that make me laugh.

Suzi Vandersteen, for fearlessly trusting her instincts and creating healing environments that change the world.

Shannon Flaherty, for telling the story of her Brazilian wax and for being so open-hearted and amazing.

Kristen Gates, for sharing her incredibly beautiful drawings, for photobombing, and for waking me up to whale sharks.

Chris Martin, for showing me what it looks like to truly surrender to spirit.

Amy Nowak, for being a philanthropist, healer, & rarefied professor.

Timothy Cope, for being such a beautiful indoctrinator of shamanism (where there is no doctrine) and for being a bona fide Heyoka.

Jeff Nelson, for dressing as Britney Spears and for defying limits.

Deanna Nelson, for having the nerve to buy a red electric guitar and play it at church.

David Thickens, for being a first responder in life to the many friends and family members lucky enough to be connected to him.

Thanks to my dear friends of The Brain Trust: *Jennifer, Mary, Suzi, Kathleen, Maggie, Lisa,* and *Krista*, for being here and there and everywhere they're needed when they're needed. (You are always needed.)

A big thanks to my family ...

to my husband Mark, for collaborating with me as a team on this giant pilgrimage of life. I love him and thank him for allowing me to be free to be me. (P.S. I know vision quests are good, but please continue to eat food occasionally, as we do have four kids to raise and that takes strength.)

to my son George, age fifteen, for mostly tolerating my outlandish and exuberant singing, dancing, mumbling, and disorderly orderliness, even though he's an adolescent. I've learned so much from his wisdom, and I continue to learn more from him and his powerful, peaceful presence every day. I encourage him to keep telling me when he has reason to believe I'm out of line. (P.S. The dishwasher needs to be unloaded.)

to my daughter Katherine, age eleven, for showing me what it looks like to be so connected to body and mind. I see how beautifully she trusts her inner self and am in awe of what an amazing friend and loving leader she is. (P.S. Thanks for pointing out when your next orthodontist appointment is so we don't miss it.)

to my daughter Josephine, age nine, for dreaming up amazing party ideas like champagne glasses on movie night, for creating amazing characters like Bling Bling, and for letting me rub her back at night.

She's a sensitive and beautiful soul who cares very deeply for people and animals. (P.S. Is your room clean yet?)

to my son Charlie, age seven, for being the scarlet macaw in our family – showing us what it looks like to be loud, colorful, and, most of all, full of love for others. I hope he continues to scream with laughter and to swim effortlessly, like an otter at Knife River, with his belly to the river bottom. (P.S. Please don't tease the dog.)

to my mom, who's been a fabulous editor, correcting grammar without trying to edit out the saltiness or the reality so as to make it all no more controversial than soft, pretty kittens. I thank her also for being patient with me when I'm a rapscallion. I am not yet fully grown.

to my sister, Maria, a comedian and amazing sister, who's been a sounding board for some of the concepts in this book and who's a textbook example of a FREAK who's doing just exactly what she's inspired to do. Thanks to her also for encouraging others to FREAK every time she does her work.

to my dad, for being another textbook FREAK and for expressing all of his awesome multitudes. Also, for reading some of this book over Mom's shoulder when it was in progress and really liking some of the chapters.

Thanks to Kim Bagwill of The Frantic Meerkat for the book's beautiful cover. Her born-to-FREAK art and products slay me and make me fall down laughing. Alice the Elephant says she really enjoys starring on the cover and finds the crown particularly appropriate.

Thanks to Matt Adrian (aka The Mincing Mockingbird), Kim Bagwill's born-to-FREAK spousal unit, for creating his insanely and hilariously titled fine art paintings of birds in the wild, some of whom are immensely troubled. I am so glad his awesome no longer lies dormant.

> Get help with your sickest
> and most kick-ass ideas,
> so they actually get done.

Thanks to Drai Bearwomyn of Wild Redhead Design for her amazing book and cover design and the wild redheaded sisterly wisdom she's shared with me, about everything from marketing ideas and connections to send-off spirit songs. I feel soooo very lucky to have stumbled into her beautifully capable hands, and I look forward to taking part in more fabulous opportunities to collaborate with her.

Thank you, dear readers, for reading. Now, off with you! **Go fearlessly and honey badger–like into the world to do what you were born to do**: shine your light, ruffle feathers, speak your truth, be loud and untamed when you're feeling it, and never forget that you (and all your multitudes) are perfect just exactly as you are.

Échale ganas,
Sarah

ÉCHALE GANAS!
(Some elephants do speak Spanish.)

Have the courage to do your thang!

" *Alice*

 sarah bamford seidelmann m.d. | www.borntoFREAK.com

MORE ABOUT

In case you were wondering ...

I live in northern Minnesota with my husband, Mark, our four awesome children, two parakeets, and one dog. I love to walk with our dog, Spirit, in the wilderness near our house, because that always feels so good. I enjoy spending time alone, doing healing work on behalf of others, coaching, throwing parties, attending parties, restyling rooms in our house, cooking good food, and listening to music (from the monks singing at Plum Village to rapper Tinie Tempah). My aim is to live my life like a very, very bright torch.

I'm a Martha Beck Certified Life Coach. I'm currently a student at the Foundation for Shamanic Studies, in their three-year program for healers, studying under the fierce and amazing Alicia Gates.

When I encourage others to be happy, I'm happy. I currently offer life coaching by phone and shamanic healing in person. If you're interested in either, please contact me directly (**www.sarah@followyourfeelgood.com**) or visit my site to learn more (**www.followyourfeelgood.com**).

This is my second book in two years. **Sheesh, I've had a lot to share lately! My first book,** *What the Walrus Knows*, is about how reconnecting with nature, and particularly with wild animals, can empower us and help us navigate big changes in life. That's what connecting with Beasties did and keeps on doing for me. I've seen the concepts I explain in the book change people's lives – especially really, really intelligent and brilliant people's lives.

What the Walrus Knows was based on work I did with others during a series of interactive podcasts (37 in all) called ***Squirrel! Radio: The Magic of Animal Totems***, during which we talked about the messages of wild animals in our lives. (**You can find and download those podcasts for free at iTunes.**) People on the podcasts kept wanting to know what I thought of the Beasties that came into their lives, so I wrote the book as a loving answer to those requests. A second edition of *What the Walrus Knows*, with an expanded collection of Beastie Manifestos, is coming very, very soon!

A ***What the Walrus Knows*** app for iPhone/iPad allows users to access a field guide to Beasties from all over the planet and see what their messages might be for the individuals whose lives they enter. The app also allows users to perform divinations for themselves, finding assistance with troublesome issues from the hidden world of spirits. **I can't wait for more humans to connect with the messages of Beasties. It's good for all of us.**

I've created many videos of my own. I love to use films to create a mood or feeling for the viewer. **You can view many of my films on my YouTube channel: Sarah Seidelmann**. Many more videos, including ones about how to incorporate spirituality into your life, are available on the site Suzi Vandersteen and I created years ago: joyjunket.com. My sister Maria calls Joy Junket "Doprah" ("a Duluth-based Oprah-like Show").

I teach tele-classes and also co-lead retreats with and for irrepressible humans, in beautiful natural places. On the island of Kauai, Hawaii, I co- lead a retreat with Susan Honnell (another Martha Beck Certified Coach) called Jazz The Glass (surfer lingo for "ride the wave"). The retreat combines surfing, stand-up paddle boarding, and hiking with shamanism and learning to connect with the web of life, the source from which all things come.

Please check my website (**www.followyourfeelgood.com**) for current class and retreat offerings and to **join my mailing list**. I send updates about every three weeks, with resources, updates about what I offer, and FEEL GOOD ideas.

I'd love to know what you think of this book and how you were born to FREAK. Send me an email at

sarah@followyourfeelgood.com

Sarah Seidelmann
www.followyourfeelgood.com

MORE ABOUT ALICE

Alice is a salty pachyderm. As an elephant, she's eminently qualified to goad creatives, mavericks, change agents, and all irrepressibles to inspired action. Elephants are known for their extensive social networks, incredible patience with members of their tribe, affectionate ways, and (at times) fierce action.

Alice loves companionship, her children, her matriarchal herd, and dressing up glamorously for special occasions, with India-inspired exotic flair. When not busy goading irrepressibles, Alice favors tromping through the forest and exploring exotic new locales alongside delightful company.

It is Alice's greatest wish that all eccentrics, irrepressibles, and change agents come out to play on the larger stage of life so everyone can benefit. She knows that greatness is not just for elephants, that we are all born for greatness.

Sarah is Alice's human companion. Sarah speaks Elephant well enough and has kindly translated Alice's commands and quips in this book. Sometimes (with extra goading) Sarah wears base-chakra-aligning undies on her head (undies designed by Alice, of course). When Sarah does this, **her energy always goes through the roof!**

To get your Kundalini to rise,
stick a pair of undies on your head.

It works nearly every time.

If results are less than satisfactory,
I encourage you to try it in
a crowded public area.

" *Alice*

Please let Alice know how wonderful she is and/or offer her kind and helpful comments to improve her salty goading. You can reach Alice by sending an email to Sarah at sarah@followyourfeelgood.com (on principle, Alice refuses to get an email account of her own).

THE INDEX

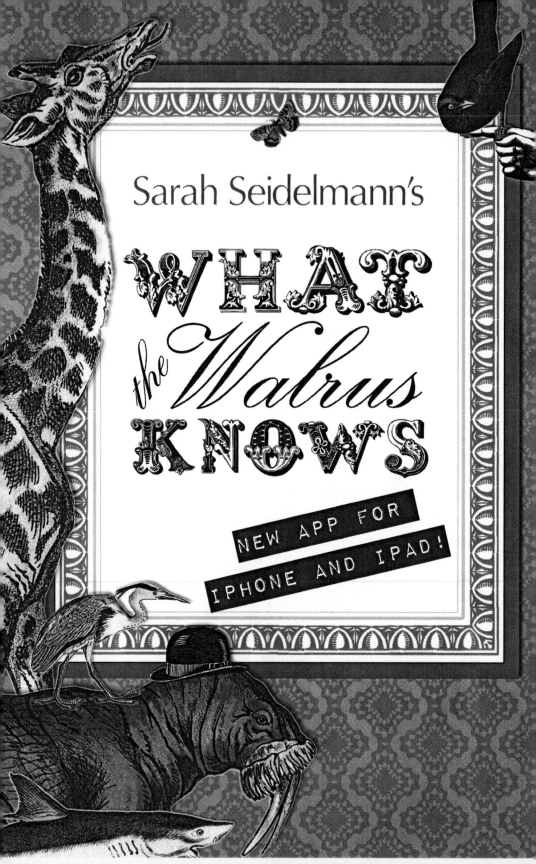

Sarah Seidelmann's

WHAT the Walrus KNOWS

NEW APP FOR
IPHONE AND IPAD!

The ancients knew:

WE ARE ALL CONNECTED.

This includes humans and animals. Beasties show up in your life every day -- each one carrying a message tailor-made just for you. A message brought by a Beastie may be about beauty or family or work. It might make you smile. It might offer you guidance on a prickly problem. Often, the message is powerful.

Connecting with Beasties messages can open the door to an amazing life. Are you skeptical? That's okay. The work and the app are perfect for skeptics. You can play around and judge for yourself, based on the results you get.

How do you get messages from Beasties? Do you have to go live out in the woods? Nope. Beasties and their helpful messages will come to you wherever you are. All you need to do is tune in. It can change everything. Curious about how? Open the app and dig in.

Device Requirements:
* 3/4/5 Gen iPhone, iPad, or 3/4/5 Gen iPod touch
* Requires iOS 5.0 or later
* Universal app optimized for display on all iOS devices
* 41.2 MB

Pricing and Availability:
What the Walrus Knows 1.0 is $4.99 USD (or equivalent amount in other currencies) and available worldwide exclusively through the App Store in the Health & Fitness category.
www.flatearthstudio.com/Apps/beasties.html

"Nature is an unlimited broadcasting station, through which [the universe] speaks to us every hour, if only we will tune in."

George Washington Carver

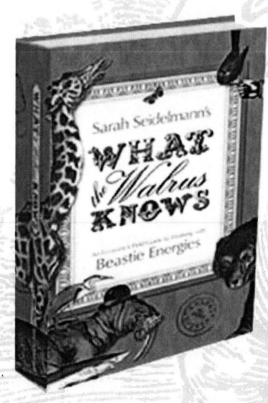

ready... set... FREAK!